How to use your Snap Revision Text Guide

This *Boys Don't Cry* Snap Revision Text Guide will help you get a top m... ur Edexcel English Literature exam. It is divided into two-pa... an easily find help for the bits you find tricky. Th... need to know for the exam:

Plot: what happens in the novel?

Setting and Context: what periods, places, ... understanding the novel?

Characters: who are the main characters, ho... ...ed, and how do they change?

Themes: what ideas does the author explore in the novel, and how are they shown?

The Exam: what kinds of question will come up in your exam, and how can you get top marks?

To help you get ready for your exam, each two-page topic includes the following:

Key Quotations to Learn

Short quotations to memorise that will allow you to analyse in the exam and boost your grade.

Summary

A recap of the most important points covered in the topic.

Sample Analysis

An example of the kind of analysis that the examiner will be looking for.

Quick Test

A quick-fire test to check you can remember the main points from the topic.

Exam Practice

A short writing task so you can practise applying what you've covered in the topic.

Glossary

A handy list of words you will find useful when revising *Boys Don't Cry* with easy-to-understand definitions.

* The 'Advanced vocabulary to improve your writing' boxes provide lists of academic terms to help you to discuss and write about some of the concepts covered in this book.

AUTHOR:
REBECCA WHITE

To access the ebook version of this Snap Revision Text Guide, visit

collins.co.uk/ebooks

and follow the step-by-step instructions.

Published by Collins
An imprint of HarperCollins*Publishers* Ltd
1 London Bridge Street
London SE1 9GF

HarperCollins*Publishers*
1st Floor, Watermarque Building
Ringsend Road
Dublin 4, Ireland

ISBN 978-0-00-847179-8

First published 2021

10 9 8 7 6 5 4 3 2 1

British Library Cataloguing in Publication Data.

A CIP record of this book is available from the British Library.

Commissioning: Katie Sergeant and Richard Toms
Author: Rebecca White
Editorial: Frances Cooper
Reviewer: Djamila Boothman (with additional thanks to Hayley Andrews)
Cover Design: Sarah Duxbury
Inside Concept Design: Ian Wrigley
Typesetting and artwork: Q2A Media
Production: Karen Nulty

Printed in Great Britain by Martins the Printers

ACKNOWLEDGEMENTS
The author and publisher are grateful to the copyright holders for permission to use quoted materials and images.
Every effort has been made to trace copyright holders and obtain their permission for the use of copyright material. The author and publisher will gladly receive information enabling them to rectify any error or omission in subsequent editions. All facts are correct at time of going to press.

MIX
Paper from
responsible source
FSC™ C007454

This book is produced from independently certified FSC™ paper to ensure responsible forest management.

For more information visit:
www.harpercollins.co.uk/green

Contents

Chapters 1 to 6

You must be able to: understand what happens in the opening chapters of the novel.

Who are the first characters that are introduced?

Blackman first introduces the character of Dante. He is 17 and is awaiting his A level results. It is clear that he is a highly intelligent individual. He has a girlfriend called Collette who texts him and wishes him good luck.

While awaiting his results, Melanie – Dante's ex-girlfriend – arrives at Dante's house with a baby in a buggy. She introduces the baby as Emma.

The second chapter in this **dual narrative** novel is from the perspective of Adam, Dante's younger brother.

Another key character in the opening chapters is their father, Tyler Bridgeman.

How is the plot introduced?

Blackman's use of Dante's **internal monologue** at the start of the novel helps reveal a lot about his plans for the future and his personality. At the end of Chapter 1, Melanie reveals that Emma is her baby and that Dante is the father.

Adam is suffering with headaches following a sports match against another school. It is revealed that Adam has a dramatic fear of hospitals and doctors.

Dante struggles to come to terms with Melanie's news. Melanie tells Dante she needs to run some errands and leaves Emma with him, despite his very vocal protests. While she is gone, Dante's results arrive – he has achieved four A-stars.

Melanie phones Dante while she is out and tells him she is not coming back. Desperately, Dante tries to call her back but he cannot reach her. As Emma's cries become increasingly intense, Dante retreats to his room. The opening chapters end with his father putting the key in the front door.

How are the central relationships presented in the opening chapters?

The relationship between Dante and Emma is initially presented as very distant. Dante uses the **pronoun** 'it' to describe her and is obviously uncomfortable in her presence.

Blackman clearly tries to create a sense of realism between the brothers, reflecting the insults and typical banter of siblings, especially in Chapter 2. Despite the insults, it is evident that the two brothers do care for one another.

Their father appears to be a strict parent. However, he also appears to put the welfare of his children first, taking time off work to take Adam to the doctor. He is also disappointed that Adam didn't tell him about the injury he received during the match.

Dante refers to his girlfriend as 'my girl'. She is also the first person he calls when he realises he cannot get hold of Melanie, suggesting he relies on her. It is revealed that, by luck, they are both planning to go to the same university and both appear to be ambitious with firm career plans.

Key Quotations to Learn

... off to university ... And a year earlier than all my friends. (Dante: Chapter 1)

'Adam, you really need to get over this phobia you have of doctors.' (Tyler: Chapter 4)

'At least you're calling Emma "her" now rather than "it".' (Melanie: Chapter 5)

Summary

- Dante is waiting for his exam results. He is expecting to do well but is clearly nervous.
- Melanie, Dante's ex-girlfriend, arrives with a baby. She tells Dante the baby is his and leaves them together while she runs errands. She does not return.
- Adam has been suffering from headaches following a match with another school. His father takes him to the doctor.
- Dante gets four A-stars in his A levels.
- Dante retreats to his bedroom overwhelmed by the events, leaving Emma crying in the living room.

Questions

QUICK TEST

1. What are Dante's future plans?
2. Why does Melanie leave Emma with Dante?
3. What event appears to have caused Adam's headaches?
4. What does Dante get for his A level results and why are they so impressive?
5. How does Blackman show that Dante is struggling to accept his role as a father?

EXAM PRACTICE

Using one or more of the 'Key Quotations to Learn', write a paragraph about how the plot is introduced in the opening chapters.

Advanced vocabulary to improve your writing

potential aspirations denial
coercion naive

Chapters 7 to 12

You must be able to: explore the significance of the relationships between Dante, Adam and their father, Tyler.

How is the plot developed?

Dante continues to struggle with his new role as a father and is clearly considering adoption and fostering as options. The complex relationship between Dante and his father is revealed through a number of tense interactions about both his results and Emma.

Again, Blackman's use of internal monologues allows the reader to see the thoughts of both Dante and Adam. The fact that a number of these feelings are not spoken aloud is quite a significant theme in the novel.

This section of the novel, especially Chapter 10, focuses on some of the stereotypes associated with men abandoning their children.

How are the central relationships developed?

On their way back from the hospital, Adam and his father argue about the tests the doctor wants him to have. Adam thinks about his mother's illness and we learn why he hates hospitals so much.

When Adam and Tyler return home, Dante tells them about his A level results. Despite achieving four top grades, Dante's father appears unimpressed. The exchange between Dante and Tyler is almost **antagonistic** and Adam is 'puzzled' by their interaction.

Tyler sends Adam out of the room in order to talk to Dante about Emma but Adam decides to eavesdrop on their conversation. Tyler expresses his disappointment in Dante. During the conversation about Emma, Dante feels very awkward about discussing his personal life with his father. Even though Tyler is clearly very angry with Dante, he phones in to work to take the rest of the day off.

Tyler sternly reminds Dante about the responsibilities of parenthood and the section ends with Adam and Emma playing together.

How do the characters react to Emma's arrival?

At the start of this section, Dante is in a separate room from Emma, highlighting his desire to isolate himself from her presence.

When Tyler and Adam return, Tyler's first assumption is that the baby is Melanie's sister. Dante tells his father that she is Melanie's daughter and Tyler figures out that Emma must be Dante's. His initial emotion seems to be anger as he glares at Dante. Tyler mentions that it is usually men who abandon their children, not women.

Dante seems to be in denial about the impact that Emma's arrival will have on his life. He is still talking about going to university and emphasises that he is not ready for the responsibility of raising a child. Dante talks about the options of fostering or adoption but Tyler insists that Dante steps up to take care of Emma properly. Tyler instructs Dante about how to hold Emma and Dante is struck by how he feels 'nothing' when he holds her.

Adam comes into the room and creates an almost instant bond with Emma.

Key Quotations to Learn

'If I had your chances, I'd be a millionaire by now.' (Tyler: Chapter 8)

'Doing a runner is usually the man's province.' (Tyler: Chapter 10)

'... there's no shame in taking any job you can get to support your family.' (Tyler: Chapter 10)

Summary

- Adam reveals that he doesn't like hospitals because that is where his mother died.
- Adam congratulates Dante on his A level results but his father seems unimpressed.
- Tyler expresses his disappointment in Dante and appears angry with him.
- Tyler discusses the responsibilities of parenthood with Dante.
- Dante struggles to feel any kind of emotion towards or bond with his daughter, while Adam's bond with her is instant.

Questions

QUICK TEST

1. How does Dante feel when talking to his father about his relationship with Melanie?
2. How does Tyler react to the news of Dante's results?
3. What two emotions does Tyler express when Dante tells him about Emma?
4. How does Blackman show Dante is in denial about the impact Emma will have on his life?
5. How does Adam react to Emma's presence?

EXAM PRACTICE

Write a paragraph analysing how the characters respond to Emma's arrival. You could then explore how their responses change over the course of the novel.

Advanced vocabulary to improve your writing

judgemental **pragmatic** **obligation** **intergenerational conflict**

Chapters 13 to 18

You must be able to: explore the key themes of identity and parenting throughout the novel.

How is the plot developed?

This section opens with Dante deciding to purchase a DNA testing kit to see if Emma really is his daughter. Chapter 13 also focuses on the relationship between Adam and Dante. Adam attempts to discuss his homosexuality but Dante shuts down the conversation, refusing to listen and calling Adam 'too young' to know who he is. Adam's internal monologue in Chapter 14 reveals his confidence in his identity. He has known he was gay since he was 13. He expresses his longing for his family to understand.

In Chapter 15, Tyler returns from shopping. He has purchased a cot, high chair, nappies and clothes, as well as food for Emma. Adam and Tyler assemble the cot in Dante's room, leaving Dante alone with Emma. When Tyler comes back downstairs he asks whether Dante has spoken to Emma. The discussion descends into an argument and Dante refuses his father's help.

As this section develops, Adam tells Dante that he is the same as his father – neither of them tell each other how they feel – and Adam **admonishes** Dante for not saying thank you.

Tyler helps Dante with Emma's bedtime routine and the section ends with Dante confirming his place at university and going to sleep, hoping to discover the day has just been a nightmare.

How are the central relationships developed?

The relationship between Dante and Tyler is further developed in this section, with Adam highlighting how similar Dante and his father are. Dante feels that his father is judging him too harshly for his mistake with Emma and not giving him enough credit for how hard he worked to achieve his outstanding A levels. Adam tells Dante that he didn't thank Tyler for the various items he purchased for Emma.

In terms of the relationships between the characters and Emma, Tyler appears to be embracing his role as a grandparent but Dante notices he is 'embarrassed' by the amount he has bought. Dante appears to be in denial about his identity as Emma's father. He confirms his university place. When he is researching about putting Emma into foster care, he feels 'sub-human' for wanting to get rid of his own daughter. He notes that children are usually in foster care because of their parents, not put into care by their parents. He continues to hold on to the idea that the DNA test will prove she is not his daughter and then he will be able to walk away from the situation. Adam appears almost envious about Dante's role as a father and acknowledges that his homosexuality will make it more difficult for him to be a father in the same way.

Key Quotations to Learn

'You're too young to know who or what you really are.' (Dante: Chapter 13)

'Nothing I do will ever be good enough for you, will it?' (Dante: Chapter 17)

Funny how that one short word could now travel so far and go so deep. (Dante: Chapter 18)

Summary

- Dante purchases a DNA kit.
- Adam tries to discuss his homosexuality with Dante but Dante refuses to accept it.
- Tyler brings the shopping home and sets up the cot and the high chair.
- Tyler helps Dante with Emma's bedtime routine.
- Dante confirms his place at university.

Questions

QUICK TEST

1. Why does researching about foster care make Dante feel 'sub-human'?
2. How long has Adam known he was gay?
3. Why does Adam tell Dante off in this section?
4. How does Adam feel about Dante's role as a father?
5. Why does Dante confirm his university place?

EXAM PRACTICE

Using one or more of the 'Key Quotations to Learn', write a paragraph analysing how Blackman develops central relationships in the novel.

Advanced vocabulary to improve your writing

hostile obstinate dismissive
oblivious inconsiderate

Chapters 19 to 23

You must be able to: explore the significance of different settings in the novel.

How is the plot developed?

In this section, Blackman contrasts the two 'worlds' that Dante is trying to exist in: the one he had before Emma and the one he has now Emma is in his life. With his father and brother unable to babysit, Dante decides to take Emma with him to Bar Belle for the end-of-term party, where he meets up with some of his friends including Josh, Logan, Collette and Amy. Logan and Josh are rude to Adam.

Initially, Dante allows his friends to assume that Emma is a relative but when Logan insults her and calls her 'ugly', Dante reacts and threatens Logan. Dante leaves the bar. It is this moment that results in Dante claiming Emma as his daughter.

Dante begins to take more responsibility for Emma. He cleans the kitchen thoroughly and thinks about all the dangers that the place poses to Emma. He calls it a 'death trap'.

What happens the day after the incidents at Bar Belle?

The following day, Adam lies to Dante about how he injured his face. Dante says that he would defend his brother against anyone, even Wolverine, and Adam questions why Dante is even friends with someone like Josh. It is revealed they became friends when Josh defended Dante from being bullied. During the conversation, Dante wonders why so many of Adam's friends are female and voices aloud his concerns about Adam, telling him, 'Different is going to get your arse kicked.' Tyler comes into the kitchen and Adam also lies to him about his injuries.

Tyler has bought baby porridge and goat's milk for Emma because they are better for her.

The postman brings the DNA kit and, a little later, Collette arrives and she, Dante and Emma go out for a walk. While they are out, Dante ends up in a confrontation with a woman in a shop, who accuses him of being a 'waster'. Another woman tries to defend him by saying that at least he is in his daughter's life and hasn't 'done a runner like a lot of men do'. Dante is angry but comes to the realisation that whatever happens, he is in a 'lose-lose situation' – society will judge him negatively no matter what the results of the DNA test are.

How is Adam's story developed in this section?

Adam's story acts as a **subplot** in the novel. In this section, we see how Adam is treated by Dante's friends in public. In Chapter 21, Josh offers to buy Adam a drink. Adam's suspicions are clear and in the following chapter we see that Adam has an injured face. There is an element of **dramatic irony** here as the reader is certain that Josh is responsible for Adam's injuries but the other characters don't realise this, especially as Adam lies to his family.

Key Quotations to Learn

'Dante, she belongs with you.' (Tyler: Chapter 19)

'... if you ever call my daughter ugly again, I'll punch your face in.' (Dante: Chapter 20)

'... you've got stuck with a kid you don't want.' (Collette: Chapter 23)

Summary

- Dante takes Emma with him to Bar Belle and ends up threatening Logan when he calls Emma 'ugly'.
- Josh and Logan are rude to Adam in front of Dante but after Dante leaves, Josh offers to buy Adam a drink.
- The DNA kit arrives.
- Dante ends up being insulted by a woman, who calls him a 'waster' for having a child so young.
- Another woman tries to defend Dante but he feels he is in a 'lose-lose situation'.

Questions

QUICK TEST

1. How does Blackman show that Tyler is thinking about Emma's needs?
2. Why does Dante go to Bar Belle?
3. Why does Dante feel that the kitchen is now a 'death trap'?
4. Why does Dante threaten Logan?
5. What happened to Adam's face?

EXAM PRACTICE

Using one or more of the 'Key Quotations to Learn', write a paragraph analysing how Blackman presents conflict in these chapters.

Advanced vocabulary to improve your writing

pivotal moment **aftermath**
conceal **prejudice**

Chapters 24 to 30

You must be able to: understand how ideas about parenthood and masculinity are presented in this section.

How does Dante cope after the insults at the shop?

Dante refuses to let the incident at the shop ruin his day and he, Collette and Emma continue to the park. Blackman illustrates how Dante is changing by showing his new irritation of people who park on the pavements – something he never took notice of before.

How is the relationship between Collette and Dante presented?

Unlike at the beginning of the novel, the relationship between Dante and Collette is now strained and they appear awkward around each other. Collette asks Dante why he had sex with Melanie but has never tried to have sex with her. Dante tries to explain that he wanted their first time together to be special and was waiting until they were at university.

Collette tells Dante she still intends to go to university and she feels sorry that his plans are ruined. Collette uses the pronoun 'something' instead of 'someone' when talking about Emma. None of their conversation focuses on his daughter.

How does Blackman introduce Aunt Jackie?

Aunt Jackie, Dante's mother's twin sister, arrives in Chapter 26. Blackman uses an **extended metaphor** of a boxing match to describe the conversation between her and Dante. Dante confides in Jackie that he is finding things difficult. Jackie reveals that she has had four miscarriages and her inability to have children was the reason for her divorce.

Tyler and Jackie also have a strained relationship. While Tyler is making the tea, Jackie asks Dante if he has told his father how he is feeling. Dante dismisses this as something women do, not men.

What happens when the DNA results arrive?

The DNA results arrive in Chapter 28 and confirm that Emma is Dante's daughter. Dante is too nervous to open the letter and leaves it in the kitchen while he attends to Emma. Tyler opens the letter thinking it is addressed to him. Tyler is initially angry with Dante for even questioning his paternity and accuses Dante of trying to shun his responsibilities as a parent.

Dante reveals that he cancelled his university place two days prior to receiving the letter.

The chapter ends with Dante encouraging Emma to say 'Daddy'.

How does Adam's story develop in this section?

Adam has started going out more frequently, spending time getting ready before he leaves each evening. He is vague when Dante questions him about his behaviour. At the end of the section, Blackman reveals that Adam is seeing someone but that this person is ashamed of both Adam and himself.

How is the central family relationship presented in this section?

In Chapter 29, Dante, Adam and Tyler take Emma to the park. During the walk, Tyler reveals that he feels 'redundant' in the boys' lives now they are older. Dante apologises for making his father feel that way and thanks him for all the things he has done to help since Emma's arrival.

Key Quotations to Learn

'It's not fair that you should have to give up on all your dreams for something that wasn't planned or wanted.' (Collette: Chapter 25)

'Of course not. Besides, girls do that – not guys.' (Dante: Chapter 26)

'Dad, you really don't think much of me, do you?' (Dante: Chapter 28)

... if he could stop feeling so ashamed of himself ... we might stand a chance. (Adam: Chapter 30)

Summary

- Aunt Jackie arrives and Dante confides in her about how he feels.
- Dante reveals he has cancelled his university place.
- The DNA results confirm that Emma is Dante's daughter.
- Adam is in a relationship with someone who is ashamed of being gay.
- The family go to the park together and Tyler shares some of his feelings with Dante.

Questions

QUICK TEST

1. What do Collette and Dante talk about while at the park?
2. Why doesn't Aunt Jackie have any children?
3. Why is Tyler so angry with Dante for taking a DNA test?
4. Why is the trip to the park in Chapter 29 so important?
5. Why does Adam feel conflicted about his new relationship?

EXAM PRACTICE

Look carefully at what Aunt Jackie and Dante say about men's behaviour. How do you feel about these stereotypes? Write a paragraph linking ideas in the text to current stereotypes about male behaviour.

Advanced vocabulary to improve your writing

grief bereaved acceptance
revelation sleep deprivation

Chapters 31 to 36

You must be able to: explain how tension is created in this section of the text.

How does Blackman present Veronica?

After a rainy walk in the park, Dante and Emma return home. Veronica, Collette's sister, arrives. Veronica is a social worker and her presence puts Dante on edge. Although Veronica insists that it is not an official visit, she asks a number of questions that leave Dante feeling uncomfortable and anxious. Veronica also says that there are a number of steps that she can take if she feels that the environment is unsuitable for Emma. Dante asks if they would be having the same conversation if he was Emma's mother, highlighting issues of gender inequality.

Veronica asks if Emma is registered with a GP. Her visit ends with her saying that a social worker will be visiting within a few weeks.

How does Dante respond to Veronica's visit?

Dante is very unsettled by Veronica's visit and he immediately phones his father. Tyler offers to come home from work but Dante assures him he is fine.

Dante phones Collette. Collette says that she told her sister Dante didn't want Emma and Dante loses his temper.

Dante makes a promise to Emma that she will be staying with him.

What happens when Dante tries to register Emma with his GP?

Dante tries to register Emma with his GP but is turned away because he does not have the correct paperwork. During the conversation with the receptionist, Dante is again struck by the prejudice he experiences as a result of his gender.

When Dante gets home, he goes through the paperwork that Melanie left with Emma. He is amazed by how much information is there and wonders what would have happened if Melanie had told him she was pregnant.

How is Adam's story developed?

Adam decides that he is not willing to be with someone who is ashamed of their sexuality and ends the secret relationship he is in. Adam is determined to live his life 'out loud' and does not want to hide his identity.

The other person does not take the break-up well and continually messages Adam to the point where Adam is afraid to turn his phone on.

What happens on Dante's birthday?

Dante turns 18 and Tyler insists that Dante and Adam go out to celebrate. Adam insists on going to Bar Belle. At the bar, Dante and Adam bump into Josh, Logan and Paul. Adam invites the three men to join them to help celebrate Dante's birthday.

Over the course of the meal, Logan, Josh and Paul get increasingly drunk and Dante is frustrated by their behaviour. Adam tries to take one of Josh's chips and Josh reacts violently, twisting Adam's wrist and calling him a 'queer son-of-a-bitch'.

The manager of the restaurant comes over and Josh, Logan and Paul exit the bar, leaving Dante with the bill.

Key Quotations to Learn

'... I know I could be a good dad if I'm given the chance.' (Dante: Chapter 31)

'Are males barred from doing this kind of thing then?' (Dante: Chapter 34)

Turn a camera on him and he sparkled ... (Dante: Chapter 36)

I wanted to do my talking with my fists. (Dante: Chapter 36)

Summary

- Collette's sister, Veronica, comes to see Dante. She is a social worker and her visit leaves him unsettled.
- Dante phones Collette and shouts at her. Their relationship is over.
- Adam breaks off his secret relationship.
- Dante celebrates his 18th birthday by going out to Bar Belle.
- Josh verbally and physically assaults Adam in the restaurant. Dante wants to punch Josh but Adam stands in his way.

Questions

QUICK TEST

1. Why is Dante so upset by Veronica's visit?
2. What promise does Dante make to Emma?
3. Why did Adam break off his relationship?
4. Why does the manager come over to the table in Bar Belle?
5. Why is Dante so angry with his friends?

EXAM PRACTICE

Tension and conflict are crucial to effective narratives. Look carefully at the key moments of tension in this section. Write an analytical paragraph about how Blackman builds the tension in each of those particular scenes.

Advanced vocabulary to improve your writing

authoritarian **conflict** **nemesis** **dramatic device**

Chapters 37 to 39

You must be able to: explain the impact the attack has on the rest of the novel.

What happens when Dante and Adam leave Bar Belle?

Dante is still angry when he and Adam leave Bar Belle. They are almost home when they are attacked by his friends. Logan and Paul pin Dante down while Josh hurls homophobic insults at Adam and pushes him against a wall. Dante shouts at Josh to leave Adam alone but Josh ignores him. Adam kisses Josh. Josh loses his temper and he violently beats Adam, punching his face and stomping on his head.

Logan kneels on Dante's back, punching and insulting him. Dante screams at Josh to stop, especially as Adam has stopped moving.

Paul releases Dante and tries to make Josh stop. He can't and asks Logan for help. When Logan stands up, Dante punches him and grabs Josh round the neck to pull him off his brother.

A neighbour calls the police and Josh, Logan and Paul run away.

What happens after the attack?

At the hospital, Dante is interviewed by two police officers. When Dante is asked if he knew the attackers, he initially hesitates but then tells them the names. Dante rings his father to tell him what has happened and Tyler says he will be at the hospital as soon as possible.

Tyler arrives and Dante tells him everything. Jackie then arrives and Tyler says Adam was beaten up for 'being gay'.

Tyler seems to blame Dante for what happened. Jackie tries to support Dante but he walks away. He blames himself. Dante thinks about the hateful things he has heard Josh say and how he dismissed them.

When he returns, Dante overhears Jackie and Tyler arguing. It is revealed that Tyler only married Dante's mother because she was pregnant. Dante makes his presence known and says he understands why Tyler treated him and Adam differently: 'Adam was wanted. I wasn't.'

Tyler immediately reassures Dante that he wouldn't change a thing.

How severe are Adam's injuries?

Adam's injuries are extremely severe: he has a broken nose and jaw, and his right eye socket has been shattered. The doctors are hopeful they can save his sight but it is uncertain.

Adam's face is unrecognisable and Jackie immediately starts to cry at the sight of him. Tyler is clearly struggling with his emotions.

Dante begins to plan his revenge.

What else happens at the hospital?

During his stay in hospital, doctors discover that Adam has a subdural haematoma – a bleed on the brain – following the injury he sustained at the sports match. It turns out he was struck in the head by a cricket ball.

While in the waiting room, Dante voices his fears that the assault will cause problems with the social workers. Tyler reassures Dante and tells him how proud he is of him. They both tell each other they love each other.

Key Quotations to Learn

'Leave now or I'll go to prison for you, I swear I will.' (Dante: Chapter 37)

'It's just a word. It doesn't mean anything.' (Dante: Chapter 38)

'... if I could go back and live my life all over again, I wouldn't change a thing.' (Tyler: Chapter 38)

Summary

- Logan, Josh and Paul ambush Dante and Adam. Josh beats Adam violently.
- The police question Dante about what happened and he tells them the names of the attackers.
- Jackie accuses Tyler of never talking about his feelings and Dante learns that he was the reason his mother and father got married.
- Adam's injuries are extremely severe and it is revealed that his headaches were caused by a subdural haematoma.
- Tyler tells Dante how proud he is of him.

Questions

QUICK TEST

1. How does Blackman show that the attack was a surprise?
2. What happens to trigger Josh's violent reaction?
3. What does Dante tell the police?
4. Why is Adam so unrecognisable in the hospital?
5. Why does Dante believe he and Adam are treated differently?

EXAM PRACTICE

The attack is a very significant event. Write a paragraph analysing how Blackman presents the incident as important to the novel. You should try to focus on the way Blackman builds up tension in the scene.

Advanced vocabulary to improve your writing

humiliation | anti-social behaviour
provocation | bitterness | malicious

Chapters 40 to 45

You must be able to: explore minor themes within the novel.

How does Dante try to get revenge for the attack on his brother?

Chapter 40 begins over a month after the attack on Adam. Frustrated by the police's lack of progress with the case, Dante tracks down Paul to ask him where Josh is hiding. Paul says Josh is staying with Logan, who lied about his grades, and that he is convinced the attack would not have happened if Logan hadn't accused Josh of being gay like Adam.

Two nights later, Dante tracks Josh down and attacks him. Josh repeatedly tells Dante he is sorry. While Dante is choking Josh, he has visions of Emma which cause him to think about the consequences of his actions. Josh then kisses Dante. Dante attacks Josh with the same sort of fury that Josh attacked Adam. Josh uses this to show that Dante hates 'us queers' as much as he does. Dante realises that Josh is gay. He also realises that the anger he felt was about the kiss and begins to question his actions.

Josh asks Dante to tell Adam he is sorry.

How does Blackman emphasise the significance of Emma in this section?

As well as forcing Dante to question his actions, Emma has a significant role in this section of the novel. The night Dante attacks Josh, Emma wakes up and calls Dante 'Dada'. Excited, Dante wakes his father to share the news.

Adam refuses to let Emma see his face, screaming at Dante to remove her from his room and making her cry.

At the end of Chapter 44, Emma comes into the room. She insists that Adam pick her up and she kisses his scars and hugs him. The action reminds Adam of his mother.

How does Blackman show Adam struggling after the attack?

Blackman shows that Adam is in 'constant pain' following the attack and reveals he has isolated himself from his family.

Adam says he is not ready to return to school and Tyler calls the doctor. Adam insists on seeing the doctor alone. The doctor prescribes some sleeping pills as Adam is struggling to get any rest. Tyler tells Dante he will keep the pills and administer them to Adam, perhaps hinting at Tyler's fears about Adam's mental health. Dante acknowledges the fact that Adam must know he needs help if he has agreed to take tablets.

Adam's internal monologue reveals how much he is struggling with the after-effects of the attack but, again, these feelings are not shared.

How does Veronica's second visit affect the family?

Tyler warns Dante to control his temper while Veronica is there. Dante is on edge during the visit but Veronica offers him a lot of useful advice. When talking about Emma's verbal skills, Dante's pride in his daughter is clear. The visit is a success and both Tyler and Dante share a sense of relief.

What does Adam tell Dante about Josh?

In the second half of Chapter 44, Adam tells Dante that he and Josh were in a relationship. Adam explains that he ended it because Josh could not accept that he was gay and used homophobic insults to put Adam down in front of other people.

Key Quotations to Learn

'You hate us queers just as much as I do.' (Josh: Chapter 41)

A life I'm too scarred and too scared to let anyone see. (Adam: Chapter 43)

'I tried to live my life out loud. What I have now isn't even a whisper. It's silence.' (Adam: Chapter 43)

She leaned forward and kissed his scar-ridden cheek … (Dante: Chapter 44)

Summary

- Dante seeks revenge and attacks Josh. During the attack, Dante learns Josh is gay.
- Adam has completely withdrawn from the family and is given a prescription for sleeping pills.
- Veronica visits the home for a second time.
- Adam tells Dante he was in a relationship with Josh.
- Emma comes into Adam's room and kisses his scarred face.

Questions

QUICK TEST

1. What lie has Logan told his friends?
2. How does Blackman show that Josh struggles with his sexuality?
3. How does Blackman show that Adam is struggling after the attack?
4. What does Emma do that reminds Adam of his mother?
5. Why are Tyler and Dante relieved after Veronica's second visit?

EXAM PRACTICE

It is important to revise minor themes as well as major themes. Make a list of the minor themes in this section, for example, secrecy and lies, and write about how Blackman presents these ideas to the reader.

Advanced vocabulary to improve your writing

vengeance	emotionally withdrawn	
reminisce	instigator	insensate

Chapters 46 to 50

You must be able to: explore how Blackman ends the novel.

What happens on Adam's birthday?

Dante goes to wake Adam up and discovers he has taken an overdose of sleeping tablets. He frantically calls for his father. Tyler tells Dante to phone an ambulance and then tells Dante to go downstairs to Emma.

Emma is crying and begins demanding to go to the park. When Dante says no, her crying increases. Dante loses his temper and shouts at Emma. He realises he is very close to hitting Emma and runs into another room.

When Emma comes to find him, he apologises to her and tells her he loves her.

Why does Dante phone Aunt Jackie?

Tyler leaves Dante at home with Emma while he accompanies Adam to the hospital. Frightened of how close he came to hitting Emma, Dante rings his aunt and tells her what happened. She tells him she is on her way.

Dante gives Emma a snack but feels that he cannot be around her and goes to Adam's room, where he reads a letter Josh sent to Adam.

Jackie tells him she is proud of him for giving himself a chance to calm down and asking for help, which she says men consider a sign of weakness.

During their conversation, Jackie puts an idea in Dante's head that there isn't a lot of information available for single fathers like him.

What happens when Adam comes home from the hospital?

Adam goes straight to his room once he gets back. Dante goes to talk to him and tells Adam he read Josh's letter. Dante asks if it was the letter that caused him to attempt suicide. Dante's question suggests he was not aware of how depressed Adam had become. Adam tells Dante that it is his appearance that triggered it and tells Dante he is scared. Dante reveals his fears about Melanie coming back and taking Emma away.

Dante also tells Adam that he is afraid of losing him and the two talk about their mother. Dante makes Adam promise he will never try anything like that again.

How does Adam feel after he comes home?

Chapter 49 reveals that Adam almost instantly regretted his decision to take his own life and shows how much he misses his mother. He walks over to the mirror and looks at his face. He says that he has 'only a couple' of visible scars and appears to be proud that he has survived. He goes to join his family for dinner.

How does the novel end?

Adam's arrival in the kitchen is quite dramatic. Tyler tells Adam that he can talk to him about anything and the two hug.

Emma then insists that Adam pick her up. Adam spins Emma around and raises her above his head, which makes her vomit on him. The other adults all laugh.

Adam quickly goes to shower and change. When he returns, Adam and Dante share the same sort of banter that they did in the opening section.

As Dante looks around the dinner table, he realises he is happy and that family is what matters most.

Key Quotations to Learn

I was less than a second away from losing it ... So I ran. (Dante: Chapter 46)

'You men can't stand to ask for help. You consider it a sign of weakness ...' (Jackie: Chapter 47)

But we were a family and we were together. (Dante: Chapter 50)

Summary

- Adam takes an overdose of sleeping tablets.
- Dante nearly loses his temper with Emma and phones Aunt Jackie for help.
- Dante makes Adam promise to never do anything like that again.
- Adam leaves his room to join his family for a meal for the first time since the attack.
- Dante ends the novel happy and surrounded by his family.

Questions

QUICK TEST

1. Why does Dante lose his temper with Emma?
2. Why does Jackie say men are reluctant to ask for help?
3. Why did Adam decide to take the sleeping pills?
4. How does Blackman draw parallels between the opening section and the closing section of the novel?
5. Why is Dante happy at the end?

EXAM PRACTICE

To what extent is the ending of the novel a satisfying conclusion? Write a paragraph setting out your ideas.

Advanced vocabulary to improve your writing

despair **regret** **overwrought**
resolution **denouement**

Narrative Form, Genre and Structure

You must be able to: understand the form, genre and structure of the novel.

What form of narrator is used?

The novel is told from the perspective of two narrators; this is called a dual narrative. The story is divided into chapters – some of which are told from Dante's perspective and some of which are told from Adam's perspective. Even though a **first-person narrative** is used in both cases, the novel features more chapters from Dante's perspective and his chapters are also longer, suggesting that he is the main **protagonist** within the story.

Using these first-person narratives allows Blackman to show the reader what the characters are feeling but also reveals how little of these feelings they voice to others. Both Dante and Adam feel very intense emotions throughout the novel. Although the reader is shown these feelings, the characters do not share them with each other. By structuring the novel in this way, Blackman reinforces the links between the plot and the title.

What genre does *Boys Don't Cry* fit into?

Boys Don't Cry focuses on Dante moving from youth into adulthood. Emma's arrival forces him to take on more responsibility and he gains maturity throughout the novel. This type of novel is known as a **bildungsroman** or a coming-of-age novel.

The novel also focuses on the relationships and conflicts within the Bridgeman family, suggesting it could also be classified as a **family drama**.

Finally, the novel could fit into the genre of **literary realism** as it contains many of the **conventions** of that genre. It focuses on a working/middle-class family and on a number of mundane or ordinary things. For example, there are a number of scenes that focus on the family having breakfast.

The genre of the text can be discussed as part of its literary context.

How is the narrative structured?

The novel features a main plot, focusing on Dante's experiences, and a subplot which focuses on Adam's story.

The opening six chapters follow a slightly unusual timeline. The second chapter, told from Adam's perspective is set a little before the events of Chapter 1, allowing the reader to see that some events are happening simultaneously.

The rest of the novel follows a **linear structure** with events told in the order they are happening, but there are a number of key moments where larger time shifts are signalled. For example, Blackman opens Chapter 44 with 'After a fortnight' and later in the chapter writes, 'Spring had finally arrived.'

How does Blackman keep the reader engaged?

The use of the dual narrative means that Blackman is able to show how characters are feeling while withholding information from the other characters. This is especially effective in the chapters where Adam is in a secret relationship and in the chapters surrounding his suicide attempt.

Blackman also deliberately withholds certain pieces of information from the reader. For example, in Chapter 28, Dante tells his father that he has withdrawn from university. The reader was not given that information prior to this event and so it makes it more shocking.

Another example of Blackman keeping knowledge from the reader is Adam hiding Josh's identity.

Key Quotations to Learn

Don't strain yourself, Dad, I thought sourly. (Dante: Chapter 8)

Today I'm thinking of my mum. And it hurts. (Adam: Chapter 24)

'... I've already withdrawn my university confirmation.' (Dante: Chapter 28)

Summary

- The novel is a dual narrative with two first-person narrators.
- The majority of the novel is in a linear structure, with the exception of the opening chapters.
- The novel fits into three main genres.
- Blackman deliberately withholds certain pieces of information from the reader.

Questions

QUICK TEST

1. How would you define a dual narrative?
2. What makes Dante the main protagonist?
3. Why does Blackman use first-person narratives for the two brothers?
4. In what ways can *Boys Don't Cry* be classed as part of the bildungsroman genre?
5. Which other genres does the novel fit into?

EXAM PRACTICE

Choose one of the genres listed above and write a paragraph analysing how Blackman uses the conventions of that genre to engage the reader.

Advanced vocabulary to improve your writing

resentment **surreal** **maturity**
paternal **cyclical**

Key Settings: Bridgeman Home and Bar Belle

You must be able to: understand how the key settings are used and presented within the novel.

What is significant about the Bridgeman home?

The Bridgeman home is the location of many of the key events of the novel and reflects the literary realism genre of the text.

Blackman uses the home to reveal information about the family. Dante sees his home as somewhere he wants to escape whereas Adam loves it, especially as it reminds him of his mother.

There are some references to the fact that the home is not as clean as it was. While Dante is waiting for his A level results, he notes that the net curtains are 'grubby' and wonders when they were last cleaned. He says that the kitchen floor 'had been a little sticky' and the work surfaces also needed 'a bit of a wipe'. Dante talks about his 'turn to vacuum', suggesting the family share household chores.

The home is also presented as significant when Dante asks what he can give Emma considering his age. Tyler tells Dante he can give her 'A roof over [her] head'. The fact that Dante can offer this to Emma highlights a key difference between him and Melanie, who is homeless when she leaves Emma with Dante.

The home reflects Dante's changing attitude towards Emma. In Chapter 15, Dante asks if it is 'safe' to put Emma on the floor. He calls the kitchen a 'deathtrap', showing how much he worries about her. Blackman also shows that Dante has used 'every antibacterial wipe … in the house' to ensure it was clean enough for her. The change in the kitchen is **symbolic** of the impact that Emma has had on the lives of the Bridgeman family. She represents a positive change with the family taking more care over their home. The arrival of Emma seems to force the Bridgeman men out of their old routines and gives them a renewed sense of purpose.

At the end of the novel, Dante notes that since Emma arrived the family are no longer just people who 'occupied the same house'. He sees them as a family in a loving home.

What is significant about Bar Belle?

Bar Belle is a popular wine bar that Dante goes to with his friends. It is where the celebrations for finishing their A levels are held. It represents the life that Dante led before he knew he was a father.

At the start of Chapter 20, Dante says the place has a 'great, lively atmosphere'. However, the description of the bar changes when he walks in with Emma. He notices the unpleasant smell of 'armpits' and says that 'every sound jarred'.

Bar Belle also emphasises Dante's changed outlook in Chapter 36. He and Adam go to the bar for Dante's birthday. The brothers meet up with Logan, Josh and Paul and the five of them sit down to eat together. Logan, Josh and Paul are drunk and throw food around the table. Dante is 'embarrassed' by their actions, suggesting he has matured beyond them. When Josh, Logan and Paul walk out of the bar following the confrontation over Adam trying to take one of Josh's chips, Dante also realises they have left him with the bill. Blackman shows Dante swearing about his friends, reflecting his anxiety about money and his need to provide financial security for Emma.

Key Quotations to Learn

... our house was special ... (Adam: Chapter 7)

'... the Bar Belle will be the same as always.' (Dante: Chapter 36)

... a feeling shared by everyone around the table. (Dante: Chapter 50)

Summary

- The home reflects the genre of the novel.
- The home reflects the impact Emma has had on the lives of the Bridgeman family.
- The home reflects some of the differences between Dante and Melanie.
- The Bar Belle is used to show how Dante has matured and changed.
- Dante's attitude towards Bar Belle changes as a result of Emma's presence.

Questions

QUICK TEST

1. How does the setting suit the different genres of the novel?
2. In what ways do the brothers feel differently about their home?
3. How does Blackman show the house is slightly neglected?
4. How does Blackman use the house to show that Dante is changing?
5. How does Blackman use Bar Belle to show that Dante is changing?

EXAM PRACTICE

Choose one of the settings and write an analytical paragraph about how it is used to reflect the changes Dante goes through during the novel. You should try to connect your analysis to the genres of the text.

Advanced vocabulary to improve your writing

recognisable **common** **motif** **realism**

Social Issues

You must be able to: understand how different social issues are reflected in the novel.

Education

Dante believes his education will give him the opportunity to have a better life than the one his father currently has. Even Tyler reflects this attitude by saying, 'I wanted you to aspire to something'. Dante also sees education as a means of achieving what he wants. He is 'looking way beyond' university, beyond education, and towards a future where he is in his dream job.

Similarly, Collette is determined to continue her education so that she can have a good career. In this way, Collette acts as a **foil** for Melanie, who had to drop out of education because she got pregnant. Melanie is shown to have almost no opportunities as a result.

Teenage parents

At the time the novel was written, the UK had the highest teen pregnancy rate in Western Europe. Teenage parents are often represented very negatively in society. These negative attitudes are presented throughout the novel. Tyler calls Dante an 'idiot' and a 'cliché', a word which has negative **connotations.** The word helps reinforce the realism genre of the novel as teen pregnancy is a relatively common occurrence in the UK. Collette's comments about how Dante will have to 'give up' his dreams also reflect the belief that having a child at a young age will effectively ruin Dante's life.

Blackman explicitly reflects negative attitudes towards teenage parents through an unnamed character in Chapter 23. When Collette says that Emma is Dante's daughter, the woman is 'scandalized' and refers to teenage parents as 'wasters'.

LGBTQ+

Boys Don't Cry was published in 2010. In the decade leading up to the publication, there were a number of notable homophobic assaults and murders in the UK. 2010 was also the year that the US Congress expanded the Hate Crimes Law to include crimes motivated by the victim's perceived gender or sexuality.

There are two homosexual characters in the novel but they are presented very differently, reflecting some of the complex issues surrounding sexuality.

Adam is openly gay. When he starts to talk about it with Dante, Dante says Adam is 'too young to know' his sexuality. Adam challenges this by asking when Dante's 'heterosexual phase' will be over. The idea that young people cannot be aware of their sexuality is often used to dismiss people who claim to have a sexual identity other than heterosexuality.

Both Dante and Tyler are worried about how open Adam is. Dante says that he doesn't want Adam to 'get hurt' and Tyler says that he has 'always been afraid' that Adam would be attacked because of his sexuality. Tyler clearly shows he is disgusted by the attack on Adam saying he thought 'gay-bashing' was a 'thing of the past'.

Unlike Adam, Josh is not comfortable with his sexuality and is 'ashamed' of being gay. He is the **antithesis** of Adam. He tells Dante he 'hates' gay people and uses a number of homophobic **slurs** throughout the novel, all of which go unchallenged by the other characters.

When Dante is trying to attack Josh in revenge for the assault on his brother, Josh kisses Dante. Dante responds violently and Josh uses this to show how much hatred Dante has for homosexuals. Dante tries to say it is not hatred but questions his own response.

Key Quotations to Learn

'Kids having kids.' (Unnamed blonde woman: Chapter 23)

'I still want to get my degree and make something of my life.' (Collette: Chapter 25)

'It's not fair that you should have to give up on all your dreams for something that wasn't planned or wanted. (Collette: Chapter 25)

'... that was nothing compared to what I'd felt when he'd kissed me.' (Dante: Chapter 41)

Summary

- A good education is widely regarded as a way of having better opportunities in life.
- Education is used to highlight the impact that having a child at a young age has.
- Teenage parents are frequently represented in a negative way.
- Adam and Josh represent two opposing attitudes towards homosexuality.
- Tyler is disgusted by the homophobic attack on his son.

Questions

QUICK TEST

1. How does Blackman reflect the idea that education is seen as important?
2. How are ideas about education and teen pregnancy connected in the novel?
3. Why does Tyler call Dante a 'cliché' for getting Melanie pregnant?
4. How does Blackman show the negative attitudes towards teenage parents?
5. Why is Josh considered to be the antithesis of Adam in terms of his sexuality?

EXAM PRACTICE

Choose one of the issues listed above and write a paragraph analysing how Blackman explores this issue within the novel.

Advanced vocabulary to improve your writing

stereotype **ideology** **entitlement** **political values**

Socio-Historical Context

You must be able to: understand how the socio-historical context has influenced the novel.

When was *Boys Don't Cry* published?

Boys Don't Cry was published in 2010. Blackman was already a highly regarded, best-selling author by this point. Despite the fact that it is a relatively modern novel, the time period in which the novel was set and written has influenced the text.

LGBTQ+ issues

In 2006, a BBC radio DJ was accused of homophobia for using the word 'gay' as a **derogatory** term meaning 'rubbish'. The BBC defended the DJ's use of language, saying it was simply in keeping with common usage of the term. This defence triggered the Get Over It campaign by the LGBTQ+ charity Stonewall. Part of this campaign was to challenge the way that the term 'gay' was used in everyday language.

Blackman draws attention to this issue by showing that Josh uses the term 'gay' in this negative way. Dante dismisses Josh's use of the term as 'just a word', reflecting the issues surrounding its usage at the time the book was written. Blackman uses the assault on Adam as a way of showing the consequences of not challenging hateful language.

Another LGBTQ+ issue can be seen when Adam says that he won't ever get to be a father as a result of his sexuality. Laws granting gay male couples the right to become **surrogate parents** were only passed in 2010.

Toxic masculinity

The term 'toxic masculinity' was first coined in the 1980s but it gained popularity in the twenty-first century. It refers to certain traits and behaviours that are stereotypically associated with men and that are considered harmful to all members of society. For example, the stereotypical view that men should not express their feelings leads to increased aggression and depression in men, which is extremely harmful.

This issue is particularly highlighted in Chapter 46 following the assault. Adam has been repressing his feelings about missing his mother and feeling isolated after the attack, hence his suicide attempt. After discovering Adam, Dante has to tend to Emma and loses his temper with her. There are a number of instances when Dante chooses anger over any other emotion.

Fatherhood

In 2001, the organisation Fathers4Justice was founded. This was in response to the perceived bias against fathers in family court.

When Veronica visits Dante and suggests that Social Services could take Emma from him, he confronts her by asking if they would be having this conversation if he was Emma's mother.

Financial stability

One of the themes Blackman explores in the novel is money. Dante is motivated to make a success of his life as he doesn't want his family to have to 'scratch for every penny'.

At the start of 2008, the UK felt the impact of a global financial crisis and in 2009 there was a sharp increase in the unemployment rate. This is reflected in the novel as Dante struggles to find employment and is forced to apply for benefits.

Key Quotations to Learn

'I'd love to be a dad someday … It's not going to happen though.' (Adam: Chapter 13)

'… because I'm Emma's dad, not her mum, I'm failing.' (Dante: Chapter 31)

… I'd never challenged him about it, not once. (Dante: Chapter 38)

… I certainly didn't want to live my life from handout to handout. (Dante: Chapter 44)

'It's a man thing, honey. You men can't stand to ask for help. You consider it a sign of weakness.' (Aunt Jackie: Chapter 47)

Summary

Boys Don't Cry was published in 2010 and may have been influenced by:

- rising awareness of LGBTQ+ issues and an increase in homophobic crime
- discussions surrounding the concept of toxic masculinity
- issues surrounding the legal system's perceived bias towards mothers
- the impact of the financial crisis which began in 2008.

Questions

QUICK TEST

1. Which century was the novel published in?
2. What aspects of the Stonewall Get Over It campaign are relevant to the novel?
3. Why is Adam envious of Dante being a father?
4. Why was Fathers4Justice created?
5. How might the 2008 global financial crisis have influenced the novel?

EXAM PRACTICE

Write an analytical paragraph that explores the influence of one of the socio-historical contexts in the novel.

Advanced vocabulary to improve your writing

cultural values insolvency
turmoil perspective

Authorial Intent

You must be able to: understand the author's intentions and aims when writing the novel.

What motivated Blackman to write *Boys Don't Cry*?

Blackman felt that a lot of literature about teenage pregnancy focused on the issue from the perspective of the mothers. Part of her motivation for writing *Boys Don't Cry* was a desire to explore the issue from the perspective of the father.

Blackman also wanted to show ideas about parenting from a male perspective. She felt that this area had not been fully explored before, especially in Young Adult fiction.

Blackman also wanted to write the novel to raise awareness of various social issues and encourage people to talk about them rather than ignore them.

How did Blackman create a sense of realism within her novel?

Blackman deliberately shows Dante struggling with his role as a father. She wanted to reflect the difficulties that all parents face when a child enters their lives. Throughout the novel, Dante frequently voices a number of concerns he has about his ability to raise a child successfully. These concerns are common among the majority of new parents, regardless of their age. For example, lack of sleep, financial worries, emotional stress and concerns about failing as a parent are all part of Dante's experiences as he struggles to be a father to Emma. Blackman felt it was particularly important to show the reality of raising a child and being a parent.

As part of her preparation for the novel, Blackman talked to her male friends to gain insight into their experiences of fatherhood. They all talked about the profound impact becoming a father had on them and their ideas about the future. This experience is something that is shared by both Dante and Tyler in the novel.

By becoming a father himself, Dante is able to develop a much stronger relationship with Tyler. He becomes more appreciative of what his father has done for him and this changing attitude reflects the increased maturity Dante gains as a result of his new role.

How have Blackman's own experiences influenced the novel?

Blackman was in her thirties when she had her first child. She felt that her daughter had a positive impact on her life but also felt that having a child was relentlessly demanding. In a similar way, Emma has a positive impact on Dante and the Bridgeman family but she demands a great deal of time and attention from all of them.

Blackman has three brothers. She noted that her brothers had difficulty discussing their emotions, seeing it as a feminine trait. This element is also reflected in the novel, especially through the title.

How is *Boys Don't Cry* similar to Blackman's other novels?

Blackman's novels often deal with the theme of prejudice. In this novel, Blackman deals with prejudice towards teenage fathers. Blackman makes frequent references to the idea that men are more likely to abandon their children or not take responsibility for them. The fact that Blackman uses a range of different characters to reflect this viewpoint highlights how common a prejudice this is.

Blackman also deals with prejudices surrounding sexuality through the character of Adam. Blackman felt that tolerance of different sexual orientations had lessened, as reflected by the regular verbal abuse that Adam endures throughout the novel. Blackman shows that Tyler and Dante deal with Adam's homosexuality in different ways but neither initially fully accept it. Their unwillingness to discuss Adam's sexuality means he keeps a number of secrets from them, which puts him in a vulnerable position. After the assault on Adam, Tyler's disgust with the fact his son has been a victim of 'gay-bashing' suggests that he has become more accepting.

Summary

- Blackman wanted to explore the idea of teenage parenthood from a male perspective.
- Blackman highlights the difficulty of raising a child.
- The novel was influenced by Blackman's own experiences with her family.
- Like a lot of Blackman's novels, issues about prejudice are explored in *Boys Don't Cry*.

Questions

QUICK TEST

1. Why did Blackman want to have a male protagonist?
2. In what ways does Blackman show raising a child is difficult?
3. Which personal experiences have influenced the novel?
4. Why does Blackman feel men struggle to talk about their feelings?
5. Why does Blackman believe tolerance towards the LGBTQ+ community is lessening?

EXAM PRACTICE

Write an analytical paragraph about how any of these contextual factors are presented in the novel.

Advanced vocabulary to improve your writing

purpose **illuminate**
misandry **unchartered**

Dante

You must be able to: analyse how Blackman establishes the character of Dante.

How is Dante presented as a stereotypical teenager?

Blackman opens the novel with Dante worrying about his A level results, an event that many teenagers go through. The idea that these results are his 'best opportunity' to make something of his life reflects the common belief about the link between a good education and a successful career.

Dante and Adam also argue in a way that is typical of siblings. Dante calls Adam 'scab-face' and says the school team must be 'Scraping the underside of the barrel' if they picked him to play. Despite the insults, it is clear that Dante does care for Adam as he shows concern about his physical health, even if he does appear unaware of Adam's emotional state.

How does Blackman show the importance of Dante's A level results?

Dante says, 'my A level exam results *were* my life', suggesting that he has hinged everything on the outcome of his exams. Dante also wants to ensure that his family doesn't 'have to scratch for every penny', suggesting that his family has experienced financial difficulties in the past.

Dante manages to achieve four A-stars, an outstanding achievement, and he is still 17. It is clear that he has worked hard for these results but also clear that he doesn't want people to know he had to put the effort in. He says to Melanie, 'I'll hunt you down', jokingly threatening her if she tells people he revised.

A significant part of Dante's motivation appears to come from his desire to leave home and move away from his father, who is highly critical of Dante. Despite the excellent results Dante has achieved, his father seems almost dismissive of them when he responds to the news with, 'So you managed to pass, did you?' The **tag question** here suggests a sarcastic tone to his words, something which Dante picks up on and immediately feels upset by.

How does Blackman show Dante's struggle to accept his role as a father?

Initially, when Dante is told that Emma is his child, he says the news hit him 'like a bullet between the eyes', emphasising his shock. He even says to Melanie, 'I don't believe you' and refuses to accept that he is the father.

When Tyler says that Emma's cot will go at the foot of Dante's bed, Dante is horrified by the prospect. He also continually refers to Emma as 'it', emphasising his difficulty in accepting her as his own.

Key Quotations to Learn

University was just a means to an end … I was looking way beyond that. (Chapter 1)

'My name's not even on the birth certificate. How can you be sure it's mine?' (Chapter 3)

I swallowed down the disappointment flaring up inside me. (Chapter 8)

Summary

- Dante is clearly a very intelligent and hard-working student with ambition.
- He has a good relationship with his younger brother.
- Dante has a very strained relationship with his father.
- It is suggested that Dante has a short temper.
- The arrival of Emma changes a great deal for Dante.

Sample Analysis

In the opening chapters, Blackman clearly shows that Dante struggles to accept his role as a father. The blunt declarative 'I don't believe you', which is almost the first thing he says after finding out Emma is his, suggests that his instant reaction is one of total denial. This refusal to accept Emma as his own is emphasised by his frequent use of the pronoun 'it' to describe the baby, suggesting that Dante refuses to see Emma as a human being, let alone one that he needs to be responsible for.

Questions

QUICK TEST

1. How does Blackman show that Dante is intelligent?
2. In what ways is Dante presented as a stereotypical teenager?
3. How does Blackman show that Dante has a difficult relationship with his father?
4. How does Blackman show that Dante struggles to accept that Emma is his daughter?

EXAM PRACTICE

Using one or more of the 'Key Quotations to Learn', write a paragraph analysing how Blackman establishes the character of Dante.

Advanced vocabulary to improve your writing

oblivious **determined**
ignorant **detached**

Dante's Development

You must be able to: analyse how Blackman develops the character of Dante.

Why could the post-results party at Bar Belle be considered a turning point for Dante?

At first, Dante struggles to accept his role as a father. One event that highlights this struggle comes at the end of Chapter 19 when Dante decides Emma will 'just have to come' with him to Bar Belle, where his friends are celebrating their results. As well as refusing to accept the fact that his life has changed, Dante goes out without her baby bag meaning he has 'no food, no nappies, no book, nothing.'

As Chapter 20 progresses, Dante's feelings about Emma appear to change. Initially, he refers to Emma as 'a relative'. However, once Emma wakes up and starts to cry, he realises taking her to the bar was a 'stupid idea' and resolves to take her home, suggesting he is putting her first over his own desires. He also publicly declares that Emma is his daughter, defending her when Logan calls her 'ugly'.

How does Blackman show the significance of the DNA results on Dante's character?

Another key turning point in the novel is cleverly structured by Blackman. In Chapter 28, the letter containing the paternity test result arrives but Dante is too focused on Emma to open it. Dante leaves the letter on the side and his father opens it by mistake.

The argument that follows the opening of the letter reveals something to the reader that had previously been withheld: Dante has withdrawn from his university place. It is significant that this event is not one the reader witnesses.

How does the attack on Adam affect Dante?

In Chapter 37, Dante and Adam are attacked by Josh, Logan and Paul. Dante witnesses the ruthless attack on his brother but is rendered helpless by Logan and Paul. Although Blackman suggests that Adam kissing Josh was the trigger for the brutal assault, Dante feels utterly responsible for what happened: 'This was all my fault.'

After the attack, Dante seeks revenge on Josh. He realises this could result in a prison sentence. Unlike at the start of the novel, Dante now feels that if he went to prison, Emma would be his 'one real regret'. He has fully embraced his role as a father.

The aftermath of Adam's attempted suicide sees Dante losing his temper with Emma and almost striking her. There have been a number of instances throughout the novel where Dante's temper is mentioned, **foreshadowing** that this will be a key element in the novel. Dante is disgusted with himself but it does help him talk to Aunt Jackie about his fears and concerns.

Key Quotations to Learn

'Emma is my daughter and I'm taking her home.' (Chapter 20)

'I've already withdrawn my university confirmation. I did that two days ago.' (Chapter 28)

'... losing my temper and almost hitting my daughter ...' (Chapter 47)

Summary

- Dante accepts his role as a father, declaring that Emma is his daughter in front of his friends.
- Dante withdraws from university before he finds out the result from the DNA test.
- After the attack, Dante seeks revenge. He feels that Emma would be his one regret if he went to prison.
- Dante losing his temper and nearly hitting Emma makes him ask for help from Aunt Jackie.

Sample Analysis

Dante eventually embraces his role and identity as a father. At the start of the novel, Dante chooses to dispose of the dirty nappy when given the choice between holding 'poo or a baby', suggesting that he sees Emma as something even more unpleasant than a soiled nappy. However, when Logan calls Emma 'ugly', the insult acts as a **catalyst** for Dante's change of heart. Dante looks at Emma and sees her as 'beautiful. Really beautiful.' The repetition and the inclusion of the **intensifier** 'really' helps emphasise how much Dante is beginning to care for his daughter.

Questions

QUICK TEST

1. Why might Logan's insult to Emma be considered a catalyst for Dante's changing feelings towards Emma?
2. Why is the timing of the DNA result and Dante withdrawing from university so significant?
3. How does Adam's attempted suicide affect Dante?

EXAM PRACTICE

Using one or more of the 'Key Quotations to Learn', write a paragraph analysing how Blackman develops the character of Dante.

Advanced vocabulary to improve your writing

family dynamic | obligation
conscious effort | vulnerability

Adam

You must be able to: analyse how Blackman establishes and develops the character of Adam.

How is Adam presented?

Adam's story is a subplot within the novel. Arguably, Adam could be seen as a foil to Dante's character. Adam appears to be Tyler's favourite and he also has an instant bond with Emma. Adam often acts as an **intermediary** between Dante and Tyler. Adam is shown to be very sociable, saying 'Good morning' to everyone when the family go to the park (Chapter 29).

Adam plans to be an actor and does not have a back-up plan. In a similar way to Dante, Adam is very ambitious and is convinced that his 'dream will become reality'. Adam believes his looks are going to be a key part of his success as he is 'gorgeous' and 'too talented to fail'.

Adam is shown as much more sensitive and emotional than his father or brother. He misses his mother a great deal, something that Dante barely acknowledges, and in Chapter 36, Adam is 'mere moments away from tears' after Josh insults him. Although Blackman presents him to the reader in this way, Adam still hides his emotions from the other characters, reinforcing the message of the title. He closes off completely after the attack and stays hidden in his room.

How is the relationship between Adam and Emma presented?

Adam bonds instantly with Emma and seems genuinely excited about the fact he has a niece, as shown by the **exclamation** 'Wow! I'm an uncle.' The first time that Adam holds Emma, she smiles at him – something that Dante finds surprising.

The relationship between Emma and Adam is built throughout the novel and it is clear that there is a genuine love between the two of them. This bond makes the way that Adam treats Emma after the attack even more significant. Blackman shows that Adam 'screamed' at Dante to remove Emma from his room and that he made her cry twice.

In Chapter 44, Emma comes into Adam's room and goes to him to be picked up. She hugs him and kisses his scars. This act makes Adam miss his mother and makes him feel isolated and lonely. It is this combination that leads him to take an overdose of sleeping tablets. He tells Dante that he felt 'jealous' of Dante for having someone.

How does the attack affect Adam?

Throughout the novel, Adam is presented as a vibrant character. Blackman uses a **simile** to compare him to 'champagne' and he is said to 'fizz with joy' around Emma. His desire to live his life 'out loud' is at odds with his family, who worry that this will result in problems. This is clearly shown after the attack when Tyler says it is what he has 'always been afraid of.'

When Adam returns from the hospital, his looks have changed so much that he asks his father to remove all the mirrors. He also believes that his aspirations to be an actor have been ruined because he has lost his looks.

Dante recognises that Adam is no longer like he was and refers to him as 'broken' and 'a shell'.

Key Quotations to Learn

'I don't hide what I am but my family don't exactly encourage me to be open about it either.' (Chapter 14)

'At least this way she won't have nightmares about my face.' (Chapter 42)

'... I'm scared, Dante.' (Chapter 48)

Summary

- Adam is Dante's younger brother and acts as a foil to his character.
- Adam wants to be an actor and is very good-looking.
- There is an instant bond between Adam and Emma.
- The attack affects his appearance and this makes Adam believe his dreams of being an actor are over.

Sample Analysis

Blackman arguably uses the character of Adam as a foil for the protagonist, Dante. Where Dante appears to hide aspects of his personality, such as wanting to pretend he didn't work to succeed in his A levels, Adam wants to 'live ... life out loud', suggesting that he is unwilling to hide any aspect of his personality.

Questions

QUICK TEST

1. How does Blackman show that Adam and Dante are similarly ambitious?
2. How does Blackman show that Adam is excited to be an uncle?
3. What drives Adam to attempt suicide?

EXAM PRACTICE

Using one or more of the 'Key Quotations to Learn', write a paragraph analysing how Blackman establishes the character of Adam.

Advanced vocabulary to improve your writing

effervescent **gregarious**
volte-face **trauma**

Tyler

You must be able to: analyse how Blackman establishes and develops the character of Tyler.

How is Tyler presented?

Tyler is the father of Dante and Adam. Dante reveals that Tyler has several phrases or 'life lessons' that he repeats over and over to them, including the statement 'Boys don't cry.'

Blackman presents Tyler as a complex character. He is a **widower** and has been raising the boys alone since his wife died of cancer. He appears to be a very caring parent. The first time he appears in the novel, he is worrying about Adam's headaches and takes time off work to take him to the doctor.

However, he is also seen as very critical and harsh towards Dante, offering almost no praise when Dante passes all four A levels with impressive results. Tyler's treatment of Dante in Chapter 8 makes Dante feel like an 'afterthought'. The contrast between the way Tyler treats Dante and Adam is a frequent **motif** in the novel and one that is only explained at the end of Chapter 38.

Why does Tyler appear to treat Dante and Adam differently?

In Chapter 38, it is revealed that Tyler married Dante's mother because she got pregnant. He had to give up his ambitions of working as an editor in films to get a job and support his family. Dante believes that his dad treats them differently because 'Adam was wanted' whereas Dante was not. Despite Dante's feelings, Blackman shows throughout the novel that Tyler is supportive of Dante.

How does Emma's arrival affect Tyler?

Blackman draws a number of **parallels** between Tyler's life and Dante's experiences, repeatedly showing similarities between the two characters. When Tyler first learns about Emma, he calls Dante a 'stupid bloody idiot'. He also emphasises that he feels 'disappointed' in Dante because he wanted his son to achieve more in life. In Chapter 38, Blackman reveals that Tyler had to give up his dreams to support his family just as Dante has had to give up his to look after Emma.

Dante finds himself repeating some of his father's **stock phrases** as he embraces his role as a father. Throughout the novel, other characters also highlight how similar Dante and Tyler are.

Tyler offers a lot of advice and support to Dante. When he goes out to purchase some baby things, he comes home with 'three-quarters … of the baby store', suggesting he is excited at the prospect of being a grandparent.

How is Tyler's character developed?

Although Tyler is seen as quite critical of Dante, there are two key occasions when Tyler prioritises his family over everything else. The first is when Emma first arrives. Tyler has already taken time off work to take Adam to the doctor and he takes the rest of the day off to get the baby things for Emma. The second occasion is when Veronica, the social worker, visits the house. Dante is clearly shaken up by her visit and calls his dad. Tyler offers to come home to support him.

Key Quotations to Learn

'I'll phone work and tell them I'll be late.' (Tyler: Chapter 2)

'At the risk of being handed my head, would you like some help?' (Tyler: Chapter 18)

... it felt great to know that Dad had my back. (Dante: Chapter 32)

Summary

- Tyler has been raising the boys on his own since his wife died.
- He has a strained relationship with Dante at the beginning of the novel.
- He offers a great deal of support to Dante, including purchasing a large amount of baby things.
- He had to give up his career dreams when he became a father.

Sample Analysis

The relationship between Tyler and Dante appears to be very strained at the beginning of the novel. Despite achieving four A-stars, Dante is given very little praise from Tyler and feels 'disappointment flaring up inside' as a result. However, Blackman uses Tyler to explore ideas of toxic masculinity, suggesting that Tyler's antagonistic relationship with his son is actually down to his inability to talk openly about his feelings.

Questions

QUICK TEST

1. Why is Tyler raising the boys on his own?
2. How does Blackman show that Tyler is a caring parent?
3. How does Blackman show that the relationship between Dante and Tyler is complicated?

EXAM PRACTICE

Using one or more of the 'Key Quotations to Learn', write a paragraph analysing how Blackman establishes the character of Tyler.

Advanced vocabulary to improve your writing

toxic masculinity

stern **exacting**

Emma

You must be able to: analyse how Blackman uses the character of Emma.

How does Emma's arrival affect the Bridgeman household?

Emma's arrival causes a massive upheaval in the Bridgeman household. Dante is forced to put his career dreams on hold to care for her. All the members of the household are affected by Emma's inability to sleep when she is teething and all of them help babysit and care for her.

Emma also acts as a catalyst for change within the relationships in the household. Although her arrival initially causes tension for Dante and Tyler, she eventually brings them together when Tyler offers advice and support to his son.

What role does Emma play in the narrative?

Emma's arrival acts as the main dramatic device within the novel. Her arrival forces Dante to accept certain truths that he previously ignored. For example, Logan's insult to Emma reveals his cruelty and Collette's indifference to Emma implies that she is quite self-centred. Although Emma's arrival has put Dante's career dreams on hold, she helps him uncover the truth about key situations.

Emma is the cause of a number of arguments between Dante and Tyler. Blackman uses her to emphasise how strained their relationship is but also to show that, despite everything, there is a strong support network in the house.

Emma also acts as a device for making the men in the household open up about their feelings, something that they all find difficult.

Dante notes that Emma is the only reason there is any laughter in the house after the attack on Adam, suggesting she is a positive influence on them.

How does Blackman use the character of Emma?

Emma is used to highlight a number of key themes in the novel, including gender inequality and stereotypes.

The fact that it is Emma's mother who runs away is highlighted by a number of characters as it is usually fathers who abandon their children.

The confrontation in the shop in Chapter 23 also highlights the prejudice associated with young single parents. The incident at the doctor's surgery in Chapter 34 also helps reinforce this issue in the book.

Emma is also used to show Dante's increasing maturity as he learns how to care for her properly and begins to embrace fatherhood more fully.

How is Emma presented?

Although Emma is presented as playful and happy, she is also very demanding. Blackman deliberately highlights the difficulties of looking after a small child to show how much Dante is having to sacrifice to care for her.

Key Quotations to Learn

'You'd give up your own flesh and blood because she's … inconvenient?' (Tyler: Chapter 10)

... she clung to my neck like I mattered to her. (Dante: Chapter 28)

Visions of Emma danced through my resolve. (Dante: Chapter 41)

...it was exactly like when Mum used to hold me. (Adam: Chapter 44)

Before Emma arrived, we'd occupied the same house and that was about it. (Dante: Chapter 50)

Summary

- Emma's arrival causes arguments and forces Dante to put his dreams on hold.
- Emma's arrival brings laughter and positive changes to the household.
- Blackman uses the whole Bridgeman family as a way of highlighting gender inequality.

Sample Analysis

Blackman uses Emma to highlight issues of gender inequality and prejudice related to parenting. Multiple characters make comments such as 'Doing a runner is usually the man's province', including minor characters such as the woman in the shop in Chapter 23. By showing this view is held by less important characters, Blackman is effectively illustrating how widespread these prejudices are.

Questions

QUICK TEST

1. Why could Emma be considered a catalyst within the novel?
2. How does Blackman use Emma to illustrate ideas about gender inequality?
3. What issues does Emma's role help highlight?

EXAM PRACTICE

Using one or more of the 'Key Quotations to Learn', write a paragraph analysing how Blackman uses the character of Emma.

Advanced vocabulary to improve your writing

catalyst dependent
dependant upheaval

Melanie, Collette, Jackie and Veronica

You must be able to: analyse how Blackman presents Melanie, Collette, Jackie and Veronica.

Melanie

Melanie is Emma's mother. She is presented as 'stunning' and it is revealed that she is Dante's ex-girlfriend. She is a smoker and says that it is 'one of the few pleasures' she has left.

The telephone conversation she and Dante have after she has left Emma with him reveals that her father didn't care enough 'to stick around' and her mother 'had to work at two jobs just to put food on the table.' It is revealed that she has been staying with her aunt who wants her to give Emma up. Melanie leaves Emma with Dante, recognising that his stable family unit offers Emma a better chance.

Collette

Collette is Dante's girlfriend. In Chapter 1, she sends Dante a good luck message and he calls her 'my girl'. He phones her in Chapter 6 when he is trying to track down Melanie. Collette is very intelligent, gaining three A-stars and an A for her A levels.

Collette seems to resent Emma's presence, avoiding talking about her when she and Dante go for a walk in the park. Collette also says that Emma is Dante's daughter in the shop, in Chapter 23, which starts the confrontation. The fact that Collette did not foresee the potential for conflict suggests she is a little naïve about the way people react to young single parents. Collette is possibly used as a foil for both Melanie and Dante as she can carry on with her original plans whereas they have had theirs disrupted.

Collette tells her social worker sister, Veronica, that Dante does not want Emma, which ultimately leads to their break-up.

Jackie

Jackie is Dante's mother's sister and quite **acerbic**, the opposite of Dante's mother: 'Mum had been honey, whereas my aunt was vinegar', though she does offer him support and advice.

Jackie does voice some stereotypical views about gender, saying that men struggle to talk about their feelings and see asking for help as a sign of weakness. She also uses a gender-neutral **determiner** when she is discussing her divorce following four miscarriages.

Veronica

Veronica is Collette's sister and works as a social worker. Although she says the visit is not official, Dante still feels anxious.

The threat posed by Social Services taking Emma away adds to the dramatic tension in the novel. However, she gives Dante valuable advice and, on her second visit, offers further support.

Key Quotations to Learn

'I love Emma too much to ruin her life.' (Melanie: Chapter 6)

'Don't look at me. It's not my baby.' (Collette: Chapter 23)

'Some get to walk away. Some don't.' (Jackie: Chapter 26)

'I really am on your side.' (Veronica: Chapter 31)

Summary

- Melanie is used to highlight the difficulties of caring for a child without a good support network. She is Emma's mother but leaves her, believing Dante can offer Emma a better life.
- Collette represents the future that both Melanie and Dante could have had if Emma had not been born.
- Aunt Jackie is an acerbic woman who still offers support to Dante. She acts as a **confidante** for Dante.
- Veronica is a social worker and represents the outside agencies that protect children. Her presence is a source of conflict and adds dramatic tension to the novel.

Sample Analysis

There are a number of significant minor characters in the novel, including Dante's maternal aunt, Jackie. Jackie is initially presented as an acerbic woman who Dante compares to 'vinegar'. In their first conversation, Dante uses the extended metaphor of a boxing match to show how much her words hurt him. Dante describes Jackie's disappointment in him as a 'Left jab to the stomach', implying her words make him feel almost sick.

Questions

QUICK TEST

1. How does Blackman show that Melanie does not have a good support network?
2. What does Collette do that suggests she is naïve?
3. Which stereotypical opinions does Aunt Jackie give voice to?
4. How does Veronica's presence add dramatic tension to the novel?

EXAM PRACTICE

Write a paragraph analysing how Blackman presents and uses each of these female characters.

Advanced vocabulary to improve your writing

revelations **complication** **discovery**
empathy **sympathy**

Josh, Logan and Paul

You must be able to: analyse how Blackman presents Josh, Logan and Paul.

Josh

Josh is one of Dante's friends and first appears in Chapter 20. Josh is 18 and appears to drink fairly heavily. He is rude to Adam and speaks to him with 'venom' in his voice. Dante challenges Josh about his behaviour after Adam leaves.

Adam questions why Dante is friends with Josh and it turns out that Josh defended Dante from a group of bullies. Even though he calls Josh his 'mate', it is revealed that Josh does say things that make Dante 'cringe'.

Later in the novel, Josh attacks Adam. Initially, Josh is simply behaving aggressively and shouting homophobic insults at Adam, but when Adam kisses him, Josh beats him violently.

After the attack, Dante goes out looking for revenge. He tries to choke Josh and Josh kisses him. Dante begins beating him and Josh says that Dante hates 'us queers'. It is revealed that Josh is gay but he is ashamed and hates it.

It is revealed later that he and Adam had a relationship.

Josh is used to represent the danger of tolerating hate speech and the difficulty some people face when trying to come to terms with their own identity.

Logan

Logan is another of Dante's friends and also first appears in Chapter 20. He is presented as someone with 'a face like a weasel and a constant sneaky, sly look in his eyes', foreshadowing the manipulative streak that he has. Logan appears to be the most malicious character, a fact which Collette highlights to Dante. Logan is also rude to Adam at Bar Belle and appears to enjoy stirring up trouble.

On the night of the attack, Logan is one of the boys pinning Dante down so that he cannot protect Adam. While Dante is down, Logan accuses Dante of thinking he was 'better' than they were because of his university plans. Blackman uses the **speech tag** 'hissed' to suggest that there is a venomous quality to Logan's words.

It is later revealed that Logan did not get the grades he needed for his university place and lied to his friends.

Paul

Paul is one of Dante's friends. He has a smaller role than Logan and Josh but there are some key, pivotal moments.

Along with Logan, Paul helps pin Dante down when Josh attacks Adam. Paul is the first to his feet when he realises how seriously Adam has been beaten and attempts to get Josh away from Adam. He is unable to do it himself and calls to Logan for help. Logan stands up, giving Dante the opportunity to punch him. Paul drags Josh away from the scene.

When Dante is seeking revenge, he says that Paul was 'the easiest to track down' and calls him a 'little weasel', acknowledging his minor role in both the friendship group and the attack.

Paul does tell Dante where Josh is but he also tries to emphasise that it was Logan who wound Josh up to the level of rage he had.

Key Quotations to Learn

Josh was an equal-opportunity hater. Everyone got it in the neck ... (Dante: Chapter 38)

'... it was Logan's and Josh's idea to wait for you guys to head home ...' (Paul: Chapter 40)

Logan was the one who'd wound us all up like mechanical toys ... (Dante: Chapter 41)

Summary

- Josh is gay but hates that aspect of his identity. He uses a lot of hate speech.
- Josh is responsible for attacking Adam.
- Logan is manipulative. He is also a liar who resents Dante.
- Paul tells Dante where to find Josh but does try to defend his friend.

Sample Analysis

Blackman uses the character of Josh as a way of highlighting the dangers of tolerating hate speech. Dante acknowledges that some of the language Josh uses makes him 'cringe' but dismisses it. He thinks about how Josh uses the word gay in a **pejorative** way and how Dante ignored the venom behind it because it was 'just a word'. By showing Josh's homophobia to have such dire consequences, Blackman is perhaps warning the reader of the need to challenge even friends if they use hateful language.

Questions

QUICK TEST

1. Why is Dante friends with Josh?
2. Why does Logan resent Dante?
3. Why does Paul try to defend Josh?

EXAM PRACTICE

Using the 'Key Quotations to Learn', write a paragraph analysing how Blackman presents and uses the characters of Josh, Logan and Paul.

Advanced vocabulary to improve your writing

antagonist **manipulative** **repudiate**
betrayal **homophobia**

Friendship

You must be able to: analyse how Blackman explores the theme of friendship.

How is friendship explored in the novel?

Friendship is one of the themes used to present the impact that Emma has on Dante's life. In Chapter 19, Blackman shows that 'a number' of Dante's friends ring him to talk about his results and discuss details of the party but he is unable to chat because of Emma. Blackman foreshadows the way that Dante will become more isolated from his friends as a result of his daughter's presence. In Chapter 31, Blackman shows that all of Dante's friends had 'stopped calling', leaving him isolated and lonely.

Blackman uses Dante's relationship with Josh to explore the theme of friendship. After Josh is rude to Adam, Adam asks Dante why he is friends with Josh. Dante reveals that Josh stood up for him against a group of bullies and that is why they are friends. After the attack on Adam, Dante's shock means he imagines Josh apologising in the morning and things going back to normal. However, after seeing the extent of Adam's injuries, Dante wants revenge.

Why is friendship significant in the novel?

The arrival of Emma means that Dante is forced to grow up quickly and this means he has to leave his old life behind. Blackman illustrates this by showing him becoming more mature than his friends but also by his friends no longer contacting him.

Although Adam's friends are not explicitly introduced to the reader, Blackman draws a number of comparisons between his friends and Dante's friends. Adam has a large number of female friends, which Dante feels is strange. Adam's friends seem to allow him to 'shine' whereas Dante has had to change to fit in with his friendship group, especially Josh. Josh doesn't like the same things that Dante does and Dante learns to like the things Josh does instead. However, Blackman also shows that Adam's friends also stop calling when things become too difficult. Following the attack, Blackman writes that after 'two or three times' of being refused access to Adam, his friends eventually stop coming round.

How does friendship link to other themes?

Blackman uses the friendship between Josh and Logan to further explore ideas about toxic masculinity. Logan threatens Josh's masculinity by accusing him of being gay and this is what triggers Josh to behave threateningly towards Adam in Chapter 37. Logan appears to manipulate Josh, making the reader question whether this is a healthy friendship.

The friendship between Adam and Josh could link to the theme of secrecy. Adam and Josh are keeping their friendship a secret as Josh is not comfortable with his sexuality.

Friendship can be linked to the theme of parenting as Dante sacrifices his friendships in order to look after Emma. Blackman uses the way Dante prioritises Emma over his friends as a way of showing his maturity but also his increasing bond with Emma.

Friendship can also be linked to the theme of family. All the friendships in the novel seem almost **transient** but the family relationships are much more secure and permanent, highlighting their importance. This importance is also shown in Chapter 22 when Dante says that he would 'do something' if Josh had hit Adam, showing that Dante values family over friends.

Key Quotations to Learn

... I learned to like his. (Dante: Chapter 22)

Why were most of Adam's closest friends girls? (Dante: Chapter 22)

It was lonely. (Dante: Chapter 31)

Summary

- Friendship is used to show differences between Adam and Dante as well as between Dante and his friends.
- Friendships in the novel allow Blackman to show the importance and permanence of family.
- Friendship is used to illustrate the difficulties of being a teenage parent.

Questions

QUICK TEST

1. How does Blackman foreshadow the difficulties Dante will have maintaining friendships once he is a father?
2. How are Adam's and Dante's friends different?
3. How are Adam's and Dante's friends similar?
4. How could the friendship between Logan and Josh be viewed as unhealthy?
5. How could the friendship between Dante and Josh be viewed as unhealthy?

EXAM PRACTICE

Using one or more of the 'Key Quotations to Learn', write a paragraph analysing how Blackman presents the theme of friendship in the novel.

Advanced vocabulary to improve your writing

indebted **assimilate** **adapt**
negate **mitigate**

Family and Parenting

You must be able to: analyse how Blackman explores the themes of family and parenting.

How is the theme of family explored?

Family is central to the novel. Although Dante and Adam bicker with each other, they are loyal and defend each other. Dante jokes that he would attack 'Wolverine' if he had done something to Adam.

This theme is also presented through the relationship the boys have with their father. Tyler talks about the need to provide for one's family, doing whatever it takes to support them. He is a widower who looks after his sons alone.

Jackie is used to present the difficulties of family life. Tyler and Jackie have a strained relationship and this appears to make things very stressful when she visits. However, Blackman shows this changing as Jackie is with the family in the final chapter when Dante says they are all happy.

Why is the theme of family significant?

Dante's strong family network is vastly different to Melanie's. Melanie's mother has thrown her out for being pregnant and her aunt is only letting her stay on the condition that she gives Emma up for adoption. Melanie recognises that Dante has a secure family network to support him and feels Emma would be better off with her father. Melanie is clearly depressed and isolated and is worried about what she'll do if she is left alone with Emma any longer.

How is the theme of parenting explored?

Blackman wanted to show that being a parent is difficult and reflects this through the struggles that all the parents go through in the novel.

One way Blackman shows this is through Dante's declaration that while his phone came with a set of instructions, there is nothing to help him be a parent.

Melanie's mother worked 'two jobs' to feed her children, showing the sacrifices parents make for their children. Tyler has also chosen a job he did not aspire to in order to provide for his family.

Both Melanie and Dante learn that caring for Emma is a full-time activity, leaving them little time for friends or personal pursuits.

Both Melanie and Dante struggle emotionally with Emma. Dante is frightened he is about to hit her and Melanie confesses that she is scared of what she might do if she is left alone with Emma any longer.

As well as showing the difficulties, Blackman also wanted to show the joys of being a parent. Dante gets to experience a number of milestones in Emma's development and each of these has a profound effect on him; for example, her first steps and the first time she says 'Dada'.

How do these themes link to context?

The novel falls into both the literary realism genre and the family drama genre. Blackman uses these themes to help reinforce these genres. For example, she couples the petty banter between Dante and Adam in Chapter 2 with genuine concern for each other.

Blackman also wanted to show how difficult parenting is and that is why Dante faces so many challenges through the novel.

Ideas about family are also linked to social issues such as prejudice. As teenage parents, Dante and Melanie both experience a great deal of negativity.

Blackman also links the theme to social issues surrounding masculinity and absent fathers.

Key Quotations to Learn

'I love Emma too much to ruin her life.' (Melanie: Chapter 6)

... *suppose I had to do this by myself?* (Dante: Chapter 19)

'I'm afraid of being a father. I'm afraid of being a bad father.' (Dante: Chapter 48)

Summary

- Family is one of the central themes in the novel.
- Melanie and Dante have very different experiences of family.
- Blackman wanted to show that parenting is very difficult.
- Blackman also wanted to show the positive side of being a parent.
- The use of these themes reinforces aspects of genre.

Questions

QUICK TEST

1. How does Blackman show that Dante cares for Adam?
2. How is Jackie used to show the way the family has changed since Emma's arrival?
3. How does Blackman show that Melanie is struggling to be a mother?
4. How does the theme of family help present aspects of the realism genre?
5. What is Dante afraid of?

EXAM PRACTICE

Using one or more of the 'Key Quotations to Learn', write a paragraph analysing how Blackman presents the theme of family or parenting in the novel.

Advanced vocabulary to improve your writing

instinctive anxiety unconditional love tenderness symbolic

Money

You must be able to: analyse how Blackman explores the theme of money.

Where is the theme of money presented?

Money appears to be a significant concern for Dante. In Chapter 1, he talks about paying off his student loan after university, showing he does not have the money to go without this support. He talks about how his family have not had a holiday abroad for a long time. Dante appears to be motivated by money.

Dante's first concern about raising Emma is that he has 'no money'. Tyler reminds him he is 'financially responsible' for Emma and tells Dante he will need to do 'whatever is legal and necessary' to look after her. Tyler's words could also reflect ideas about masculinity and the traditional role of fathers as breadwinners for their families.

How is money significant within the novel?

When Tyler goes to buy some essential things for Emma, he returns with significantly more items than expected. Dante makes a comment that they 'must've cost a fortune'. Tyler appears 'embarrassed' that he spent so much. Here, Blackman reflects both Tyler's willingness to support Dante and his excitement at having Emma in his life.

Money is also significant in Dante's choice to spend a large proportion of his savings on a DNA test to confirm whether or not he is Emma's father.

Blackman reveals that Tyler paid for the family to go on holiday but the boys ignored him once they got to the resort. Dante uses the word 'cheapo' to show his negative attitude towards this type of trip.

Where does money link to other themes?

Money and prejudice are linked together when Dante is accused of being a 'waster' relying on state handouts to raise his child. The woman in the shop says she is entitled to her opinion as it is her 'tax money' that Dante is using.

Money and friendship are linked together in Chapter 36. The events in this chapter make Dante question his friendship with Josh, Logan and Paul. When they walk out of the restaurant without paying, Dante's harsh insult suggests that he has truly grown apart from them.

Money and masculinity are linked together when Dante shows that he has 'Too much pride' to try to claim more than just the basic benefit.

How does money link to the characters within the novel?

Tyler spends a considerable amount of money to provide for Emma. Here, Blackman emphasises the difference between Melanie and Dante. Melanie is clearly struggling and has no support network. Her family has kicked her out of the home and her aunt will only let her live with her if she gives Emma up for adoption. Melanie has no qualifications, so her career opportunities are even more limited than Dante's. This comparison allows Blackman to create a sense of understanding about why Melanie abandoned Emma.

Money is also used to show the changing priorities and attitudes Dante has. At the beginning of the novel, he feels that money is important but at the end of the novel, he recognises that being happy and surrounded by family is all that matters.

How does money link to the context of the novel?

In 2008, the UK experienced the impact of a global financial crisis. Unemployment figures rose sharply as a result. Money was clearly a concern for a lot of people and this is reflected in the constant worries that Dante has about both money and how he is going to provide for his daughter.

Key Quotations to Learn

'Dad, I've no money, no job, no way of looking after it.' (Dante: Chapter 10)

'It's my business when it's my tax money that's providing your child benefit and Jobseeker's Allowance ...' (Woman in shop: Chapter 23)

Summary

- Dante is very motivated by money in the beginning.
- Money is a recurring motif throughout the novel.
- Money is used to highlight Dante's changing attitudes.

Questions

QUICK TEST

1. How does Blackman show Dante is motivated by money?
2. How does Blackman show Dante is worried about money?
3. Why is Tyler spending so much on Emma significant?
4. Why does the woman in the shop feel she is entitled to judge Dante?
5. How does the theme of money link to context?

EXAM PRACTICE

Using one or more of the 'Key Quotations to Learn', write a paragraph analysing how Blackman presents the theme of money in the novel.

Advanced vocabulary to improve your writing

fiscal | social justice | inequality
economic | budget

Identity

You must be able to: analyse how Blackman explores the theme of identity.

Gender

Blackman deliberately wanted to focus on a male perspective for this narrative as she felt it was one that had not been explored in much detail. Therefore, masculinity could also be considered a key theme on its own as well as part of gender identity. Blackman does illustrate some stereotypes associated with a masculine identity. There are frequent references to men abandoning their children and male characters struggling to express their feelings.

Tyler uses the controversial phrase 'man up' to encourage Dante to accept responsibility for Emma. This phrase is associated with the idea of men not being able to show their feelings and adopting a practical approach to a problem.

Blackman uses this theme to expose gender inequality. Dante regularly feels people are judging him based on his gender, for example, during Veronica's first visit and when he takes Emma to the doctor to get her registered.

Aspirations

Both Dante and Adam have career aspirations that form part of their identity. These aspirations have to change by the end of the novel.

Dante dreams of becoming a journalist. Emma's arrival puts a hold on his dreams. However, at the end of Chapter 47, Dante appears to have the idea of writing some information to help young single fathers. His aspirations have changed but his motivation and drive are still there.

Adam dreams of becoming an actor. He is confident he will succeed and has no back-up plan. However, the injuries he sustains in the attack severely affect the way he looks, and he believes his dreams are over. Dante tries to reassure him that it is not too late to choose a new path.

Sexuality

While Adam accepts his sexuality as part of his identity, Josh does not. Blackman deliberately keeps Josh's identity as Adam's secret boyfriend from the reader, simply using the pronoun 'he' when discussing the man he has met. This may reflect the belief that coming out as gay is something that should only be done by the person themselves, not anyone else.

The reader learns at the end of the novel that Tyler accepts Adam's sexuality and Dante does begin to accept that part of Adam's identity but it is difficult for them both.

Age

Another key element of identity is the age of the characters. At 17, Dante's ability to go out with his friends and behave like a normal teenager seems to have been ruined by Emma's arrival. Importantly, however, Dante is happier than ever at the end of the text.

The fact that Dante is a teenager is also the source of the confrontation in the shop when the woman sneers about 'Kids having kids'.

Dante turns 18 during the novel. In terms of legal aspects of society, being 18 represents an arrival into adulthood. Dante turns 18 on the day of the attack on his brother, which corresponds with the realisation that he is more mature than his friends.

Race

In Chapter 38, Blackman reveals that Dante is black. The way that she reveals it helps emphasise that it is not a significant part of the story, as it is simply part of Dante's thoughts about how Josh is an 'equal-opportunity hater'. Blackman may also have included this subtle reference to race to challenge the pervasive negative stereotype surrounding absent black fathers – a stereotype that has been widely criticised yet still persists in a lot of modern day representations of black families.

Key Quotations to Learn

'... girls do that – not guys.' (Dante: Chapter 26)

'Are males barred from doing this kind of thing then?' (Dante: Chapter 34)

... God only knew what Josh said about me and other black people behind my back. (Dante: Chapter 38)

Summary

Blackman explores many aspects of identity:

- Ideas about masculinity and gender reflect the stereotypes about masculinity while also challenging the prejudice surrounding single fathers.
- Both Dante and Adam are very ambitious but both have to change their plans.
- Sexual identity and different attitudes towards homosexuality are explored throughout.
- Dante's identity as a teenager is important and reflects ideas about prejudice.

Questions

QUICK TEST

1. What masculine stereotypes are presented in the novel?
2. Why is the phrase 'man up' considered to be controversial?
3. What career path does Adam want to follow?
4. Why does Adam think he cannot be an actor?
5. Why do you think Blackman reveals Dante's race the way she did?

EXAM PRACTICE

Using one or more of the 'Key Quotations to Learn', write a paragraph analysing how Blackman presents the theme of identity in the novel.

Advanced vocabulary to improve your writing

esteem **regard**
perception **representation**

Secrecy

You must be able to: analyse how Blackman explores the theme of secrecy in the novel.

Where is secrecy presented?

Throughout the novel, Blackman frequently makes links between keeping secrets and misery.

Melanie has kept the secret of her pregnancy from Dante for just over a year and a half. The fact that Melanie hid her pregnancy links to the associated shame of falling pregnant as a teenager. Melanie also keeps her location a secret from Dante meaning he is left with Emma and has no way of finding her.

Adam keeps the relationship he has with Josh a secret from his family. Josh's sexuality is kept a secret until the latter part of the novel. Unlike Adam, Josh is not openly gay. He hates his sexual identity. Josh tries to cover up his secret through the violent assault on Adam.

Arguably, the male members of the Bridgeman family keep their emotions secret from each other. Dante confesses to his aunt that he is scared he will fail but he struggles to share this with his father. Adam keeps the fact he misses his mother a secret from his family, to the point where Dante accuses him of not missing her at all.

One significant family secret is that Tyler married Dante's mother out of obligation.

Jackie also keeps the secret about her multiple miscarriages from Dante until he asks her why she doesn't have children.

How does secrecy link to other themes?

Secrecy and parenting are linked in the text. Melanie keeps her role as a parent a secret and Tyler keeps secret about how he became a parent as well. These secrets impact dramatically on Dante.

Secrecy is linked to the theme of family. Initially, all the male members of the Bridgeman family keep secrets from one another. However, as the novel progresses, they begin to confide in one another more easily. Blackman uses this to show how the family changes due to Emma's arrival. For example, in Chapter 48, Dante tells Adam that he is 'afraid' of not being able to support Emma and that Melanie will come back and take Emma away.

Josh keeps his sexual identity a secret as he believes it affects his masculine identity. Josh is ashamed of his sexuality and keeps it from his friends, linking the theme of secrecy to the theme of friendship.

How is secrecy linked to context?

Melanie hiding her pregnancy reflects the **stigma** surrounding teenage pregnancy. This is reinforced by the fact that her mother threw her out of the house and that her aunt expects her to give Emma up for adoption. There were a huge number of cases where women were hidden away to give birth and then had their babies taken from them to be adopted.

The fact that Melanie's experience seems to echo elements of this practice builds sympathy for the character and allows Blackman to suggest things have not progressed as much as people think they have.

The fact that Josh is afraid to be open about his sexuality also links to the lack of progress Blackman felt that the LGBTQ+ movement had made in terms of increasing tolerance and acceptance in society.

Key Quotations to Learn

I immediately tried to re-call her but her number was blocked. (Dante: Chapter 6)

He wants to keep his true self hidden away ... (Adam: Chapter 33)

'... you only married Mum because she was pregnant … with me.' (Dante: Chapter 38)

Summary

There are a number of secrets that are revealed throughout the novel:

- Melanie's pregnancy
- Josh's sexuality
- Tyler marrying Dante's mother out of obligation
- the relationship between Josh and Adam.

The Bridgeman men keep their emotions a secret from each other.

Questions

QUICK TEST

1. Why does Melanie keep the pregnancy a secret from Dante?
2. In what way does Blackman use the theme of secrecy to show the difference between Adam and Josh?
3. In what ways does the theme of secrecy link to other themes?
4. What evidence does Blackman offer to show there is a stigma around teenage pregnancy?
5. What evidence is there that Blackman feels the LGBTQ+ movement has not made as much progress as people think?

EXAM PRACTICE

Using one or more of the 'Key Quotations to Learn', write a paragraph analysing how Blackman presents the theme of secrecy in the novel.

Advanced vocabulary to improve your writing

withhold conceal
omission disclosure

Tips and Assessment Objectives

You must be able to: understand how to approach the exam question and meet the requirements of the mark scheme.

Quick Tips

- You will get a choice of two questions. You only need to answer one of them.
- Remember that there are a number of texts available for this part of the exam paper so you may have to flip through the question booklet to find the *Boys Don't Cry* section.
- You will be given a question linked to a short quotation from the novel. You **do not** need to use the quotation in your response. Just make sure you focus on the question.
- Make sure you know what the question is asking you. Underline key words and use the prompt at the bottom that reminds you to include context in your answer.
- You should spend about 50 minutes on your *Boys Don't Cry* response. Remember that 20% of the marks for this question (8/40) are awarded for your spelling, punctuation and grammar so it is vital that you leave yourself time to proofread your work carefully.
- Give yourself about 5–10 minutes to plan so that your essay has a secure structure.
- It can sometimes help, after each paragraph or point, to quickly re-read the question to keep yourself focused on the exam task.
- As context is worth so many marks in this question, it is vital that you discuss what the writer's intentions were when they wrote the novel.
- Keep your writing concise. If you waste time 'waffling', you won't be able to show the breadth and depth of ideas that the mark scheme requires.

AO1: Maintain a critical style and develop an informed personal response supported by relevant references

You need to be able to structure a secure argument that engages with the text and the question. You will need to incorporate quotations and references from across the novel. You will also need to write in a formal, academic style.

Lower	Middle	Upper
A narrative style of essay with some references to the text. Style loses focus in places and does not maintain tone.	Response has a secure structure and presents a clear argument that is focused on the question. Style is appropriate; includes some supporting references.	Response is assured and confident with precisely selected references to support ideas. Essay has convincing and perceptive style.

AO3: Show understanding of the relationships between texts and the contexts in which they were written

You need to be able to discuss how the context of the novel has influenced the content and style. You also need to look at what Blackman was trying to achieve in terms of the aims of the novel. You should also consider the context within the novel. For example, the family relationships between the three main male characters or Dante's age.

Lower	Middle	Upper
Some comment about context although not always focused on the question. Some attempt to link the context and the novel together.	Secure discussion about context with relevant focused links between context and the text.	Excellent understanding of the influence of context. Links between context and the text are perceptive and integrated into the main body of the essay.

AO1 and AO3 are marked together and are worth a total of **32 marks**.

AO4: Use a range of vocabulary and sentence structures for clarity, purpose and effect, with accurate spelling and punctuation (8 marks)

You need to ensure your essay is well-structured and that you have used a good range of vocabulary, sentence structures, and punctuation. To help you build your vocabulary and increase the critical style of your responses, there are a number of useful words and phrases in the 'Advanced vocabulary' boxes that appear across the bottom of earlier pages in this book. You could practise incorporating these terms into your essays. You should also ensure that your essay is paragraphed clearly. Look carefully at the language of the question to ensure you spell all of the words used there correctly.

Lower	Middle	Upper
A reasonable range of vocabulary and punctuation that is generally accurate. Some variety of sentence structure and punctuation.	Spelling and punctuation is considerably accurate. There is a considerable range of vocabulary and sentence structures. Writing is controlled.	A broad range of vocabulary and punctuation that is used almost flawlessly. Sentence structure adds to the meaning and is used for effect. Writing is controlled and sophisticated.

Practice Questions

Character questions

Some of the exam questions will specifically ask you to focus on a character and their significance within the novel. You should think about how and why Blackman uses the characters she has created. Think about what they symbolise or represent.

Before Emma arrived, we'd occupied the same house and that was about it. (Dante)

In what ways is Emma important in *Boys Don't Cry*?

You **must** refer to the context of the novel in your answer.

[40 marks] (includes 8 marks for the range of appropriate vocabulary and sentence structures, and accurate use of spelling and punctuation)

Mum had been honey, whereas my aunt was vinegar. (Dante)

Explore the significance of the character of Aunt Jackie in *Boys Don't Cry.*

You **must** refer to the context of the novel in your answer.

[40 marks] (includes 8 marks for the range of appropriate vocabulary and sentence structures, and accurate use of spelling and punctuation)

Changing characters

Other character questions will ask you to look at how a character changes over the course of the novel. In these questions you need to ensure you are covering the story without simply retelling it.

I racked my brains for some way to help my brother, for some way to get the real Adam back ... (Dante)

How does Adam change throughout the novel?

You **must** refer to the context of the novel in your answer.

[40 marks] (includes 8 marks for the range of appropriate vocabulary and sentence structures, and accurate use of spelling and punctuation)

Relationships

Character questions might also ask you to focus on relationships within the novel. You will need to look at why these relationships are important to both the narrative and Blackman's intentions.

'Why are you friends with him? And that Logan is even worse.' (Adam)

Explore the significance of Dante's relationship with his friends.

You **must** refer to the context of the novel in your answer.

[40 marks] (includes 8 marks for the range of appropriate vocabulary and sentence structures, and accurate use of spelling and punctuation)

Themes

You might also be asked a theme-based question. You need to be able to explore how the theme is presented in the novel and why it is significant – both to the plot and Blackman's intentions.

'You should've let me pummel him.' I was still fuming as Adam and I walked home. (Dante)

Explore the significance of anger in *Boys Don't Cry.*

You **must** refer to the context of the novel in your answer.

[40 marks] (includes 8 marks for the range of appropriate vocabulary and sentence structures, and accurate use of spelling and punctuation)

'Doing a runner is usually the man's province, not the woman's.' (Tyler)

Explore how ideas about masculinity are important in the novel.

You **must** refer to the context of the novel in your answer.

[40 marks] (includes 8 marks for the range of appropriate vocabulary and sentence structures, and accurate use of spelling and punctuation)

'Whether you give her up or keep her, your world has now changed and it's going to stay that way.' (Tyler)

Explore the significance of change within the novel.

You **must** refer to the context of the novel in your answer.

[40 marks] (includes 8 marks for the range of appropriate vocabulary and sentence structures, and accurate use of spelling and punctuation)

Practice Questions

Minor themes

Remember, you could be asked to explore relatively minor themes. It is important you know the text really well so that you can draw on many different elements in your response.

'At the risk of being handed my head, would you like some help?' (Tyler)

In what ways is helping others important in the novel?

You **must** refer to the context of the novel in your answer.

[40 marks] (includes 8 marks for the range of appropriate vocabulary and sentence structures, and accurate use of spelling and punctuation)

Unusual questions

You might also be asked more unusual questions that do not explicitly ask you to explore a character or theme.

Boys don't cry – that's what Dad had always told me and my brother. (Dante)

Explore the significance of the title of the novel.

You **must** refer to the context of the novel in your answer.

[40 marks] (includes 8 marks for the range of appropriate vocabulary and sentence structures, and accurate use of spelling and punctuation)

Like a well-worn but comfortable coat, our house was special in a way that wasn't immediately obvious. (Adam)

Explore the significance of the settings in *Boys Don't Cry.*

You **must** refer to the context of the novel in your answer.

[40 marks] (includes 8 marks for the range of appropriate vocabulary and sentence structures, and accurate use of spelling and punctuation)

Revision tips

If you look at all the questions above, you will notice that they have a fairly similar style in terms of how they are written. A lot of exam questions will follow this idea of a 'stem sentence' – a common pattern – to ensure that questions are equal year after year. This means that you could easily write your own questions to help your revision.

You could also try to create your own mark schemes for your questions. This will enable you to really think about the demands of the exam without producing more essays. Try to incorporate some of the advanced vocabulary from the boxes at the bottom of earlier pages in this book.

Summary

- You need to be prepared to answer questions on characters, themes and issues within the novel.
- You must ensure you have a secure understanding of what Blackman's intentions were when writing the novel.
- Exam questions usually follow a predictable stem that you can recreate in your own questions.

Planning a Character Question Response

You must be able to: understand what an exam question is asking you and prepare your response.

How might an exam question be phrased?

Remember that exam questions usually follow a typical structure. For example, a character question might look like this:

> *... it felt great to know that Dad had my back.* (Dante)
>
> Explore the significance of Tyler within the novel.
>
> You **must** refer to the context of the novel in your answer.
>
> [40 marks] (includes 8 marks for the range of appropriate vocabulary and sentence structures, and accurate use of spelling and punctuation)

Remember that the quotation is there as a prompt. You do not need to incorporate it into your essay if it doesn't fit your plan.

How do I work out what to do?

The first thing to remember is the assessment objectives. You are going to be assessed on your ability to construct a logical and well-supported argument (AO1) that also integrates context (AO3) into the response. Remember that context can include the social and historical context of the novel, the writer's intentions, and the context of the novel itself.

You need to identify at least four or five points about the focus of the question that you can cover in the 50 minutes you have in the exam.

As you will need time to both plan and proofread, you will probably be writing for about 35–40 minutes. You will not have time to write about everything that a character does or every time a theme is shown. Remember that the accuracy of your writing is also assessed (AO4) so proofreading your response is essential.

How do I prepare for a character question?

For character questions, you need to think about what the characters symbolise or represent beyond their role in the novel. For the example above, you need to think about what Tyler represents in terms of the way he reflects ideas about responsibility, masculinity and family.

Because you are also being assessed for AO3, you need to link this to the author's intentions. You also need to think about the context within the novel. For example, the fact that Tyler is so repressive of his emotions means that his sons do the same thing.

How do I write my response?

Your response needs to be a **cohesive** essay that is fully focused on the question. When putting your plan together, you need to make sure that you are thinking about the order of ideas as well as the content.

What should my plan look like?

Planning can be quite individual, so you need to work out a method that works for you. One option is to produce a spider diagram of all the ideas you have about the question:

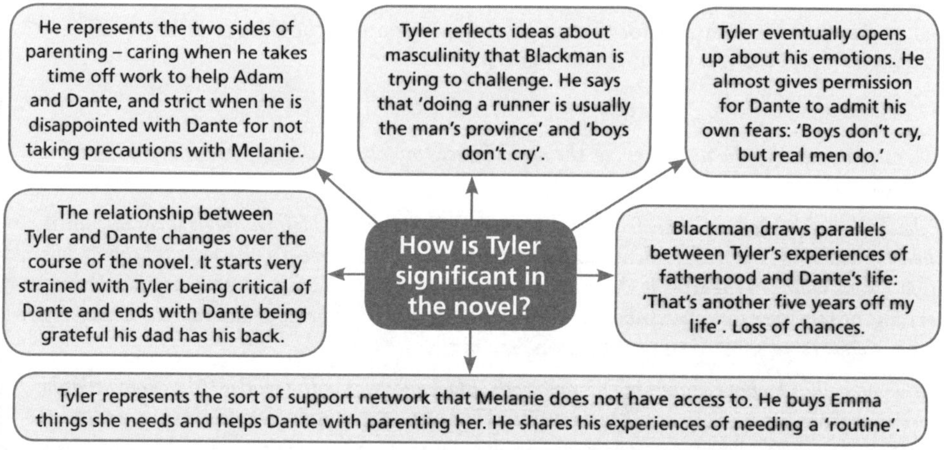

How is Tyler significant in the novel?

- He represents the two sides of parenting – caring when he takes time off work to help Adam and Dante, and strict when he is disappointed with Dante for not taking precautions with Melanie.
- Tyler reflects ideas about masculinity that Blackman is trying to challenge. He says that 'doing a runner is usually the man's province' and 'boys don't cry'.
- Tyler eventually opens up about his emotions. He almost gives permission for Dante to admit his own fears: 'Boys don't cry, but real men do.'
- The relationship between Tyler and Dante changes over the course of the novel. It starts very strained with Tyler being critical of Dante and ends with Dante being grateful his dad has his back.
- Blackman draws parallels between Tyler's experiences of fatherhood and Dante's life: 'That's another five years off my life'. Loss of chances.
- Tyler represents the sort of support network that Melanie does not have access to. He buys Emma things she needs and helps Dante with parenting her. He shares his experiences of needing a 'routine'.

Once you have the ideas written down, you could then number them so you know the order that you are going to follow. This will help you produce a fluent and cohesive essay. You also need to make sure you have context interwoven with all of your points.

Summary

- Make sure you know what the focus of the question is.
- Make sure you are able to discuss what the character represents both within the novel and in wider society.
- Make sure you think about the order of your points to help produce a cohesive essay.
- Make sure you integrate context into every point.

Questions

1. Which three assessment objectives are you tested on in this exam?
2. What things can you write about to cover context?
3. Why is it so important to proofread your answer?

Grade 5 Annotated Response to a Character Question

... it felt great to know that Dad had my back. (Dante)

Explore the significance of Tyler within the novel.

You **must** refer to the context of the novel in your answer.

[40 marks] (includes 8 marks for the range of appropriate vocabulary and sentence structures, and accurate use of spelling and punctuation)

Tyler is the father in the novel and, as the novel focuses on fathers, this shows he is an important character (1).

Tyler has trouble expressing his feelings in the novel. He doesn't (2) tell Dante he loves him until the very end of the book (3) and he also tells his sons that 'boys don't cry'. Because Blackman has used Tyler's words in the title, it shows that he is an important character. Also, when Blackman was writing, people were concerned about toxic masculinity and this phrase is an example of that. Tyler seems to represent some ideas about toxic masculinity (4).

Although he has trouble expressing his emotions, Blackman wants the reader (5) to know that he does care about his sons. Tyler takes time off work to ensure that Adam visits a doctor, and then takes the rest of the day off to support Dante when Emma is left with him. Tyler also purchases a great deal of baby items for Emma's benefit even though the family do not have a lot of money. This shows the reader that Tyler is very supportive and shows that Emma might be well looked after if Dante and Tyler can work together (6).

Tyler also offers advice about how to care for Emma even though he and Dante argue. Tyler says, 'At the risk of being handed my head, would you like some help?' showing he just wants to help his son. Blackman may have done this to show that fathers can be caring and that Tyler is a good father to Dante. There are a lot of negative representations of single fathers in the media and by showing Tyler in this positive way, Blackman is challenging those ideas (7).

Tyler is not a perfect father though. (8) He is not very kind when Dante gets his A level results saying, 'So you managed to pass, did you?' which seems sarcastic. He does not seem very proud of Dante at the beginning of the novel. This changes at the end of the novel though when Tyler not only says that he is proud of Dante but also that he loves him 'very much'. This is important (9) as it shows that Tyler has changed from being unable to express himself to being able to tell Dante how he feels. This change suggests that it is important for men to be able to share their emotions as it makes Dante feel better even though he nearly lost his brother.

Overall, Tyler is important as he is a positive presentation of single fathers, which is something that Blackman was trying to achieve, and he shows how important it is for men to be able to share their emotions (10).

1. Clear opening that links to the question (AO1) and offers a simple comment about the context of the novel (AO3).
2. Informal language, such as **contractions**, should be avoided where possible in these essays. (AO4)
3. Range of references to support ideas. (AO1)
4. Although the AO3 is not as smoothly integrated as it could be, there are valid comments about Tyler and what he represents. It also remains focused on the question. (AO1)
5. Explicit reference to the writer's intentions. (AO3)
6. Personal response and interpretation of the events in the novel. (AO1)
7. Contextual ideas are included but they are slightly less integrated than in higher responses. (AO3)
8. Strong personal response (AO1) and some attempt to use a variety of sentence structures for effect. (AO4)
9. Another link to the question to help maintain focus. (AO1)
10. Conclusion offers a summary of the main ideas of the essay.

Questions

EXAM PRACTICE

Choose a paragraph or section from this essay. Read it through a few times then try to rewrite and improve it. You might:

- improve the sophistication of the language or the clarity of expression
- integrate the contextual points more fluently
- try to increase the range of punctuation and variety of sentence structures.

Then try to identify one more point that could be included in the essay to develop and support the ideas further.

Grade 7+ Annotated Response to a Character Question

A proportion of the best top-band answers will be awarded Grade 8 or Grade 9. To achieve this, you should aim for a sophisticated, fluent and nuanced response that displays flair and originality.

... it felt great to know that Dad had my back. (Dante)

Explore the significance of Tyler within the novel.

You **must** refer to the context of the novel in your answer.

[40 marks] (includes 8 marks for the range of appropriate vocabulary and sentence structures, and accurate use of spelling and punctuation)

Tyler is extremely significant within the novel as Blackman uses him to represent ideas about both masculinity and parenting, two of the key themes within the text (1).

The concept of toxic masculinity was frequently debated at the time of publication and, like many of her novels, Blackman incorporated this socio-political theme into the story, not only to challenge the ideas but also to emphasise the realism of her work (2). Tyler represents the effects of many aspects of toxic masculinity. He appears to have trouble expressing his feelings towards his sons and even goes so far as to tell them that 'boys don't cry'. By making the title of the novel one of Tyler's stock phrases, and a phrase commonly associated with issues surrounding toxic masculinity, Blackman effectively illustrates just how important both Tyler and this theme are to the narrative (3).

Although he has trouble expressing his emotions, Blackman ensures that there is no doubt about whether Tyler cares for his sons. The first significant action that Tyler completes within the novel is to take time off work to ensure that Adam visits a doctor, reflecting the idea that Tyler puts his children first above his own professional and financial needs. Blackman continues to reinforce this impression of Tyler when he takes the rest of the day off to support Dante and purchases a large number of baby items for Emma's benefit, taking over some of the practical aspects of Emma's care. Tyler's actions exaggerate the difference between Dante's situation and Melanie's: Dante has a support network that Melanie does not, creating sympathy for the character (4).

Despite there being obvious conflict between Tyler and Dante, Tyler never refuses to help his son in terms of offering advice about how to care for Emma. At one point, Tyler says, 'At the risk of being handed my head, would you like some help?', suggesting that even though he knows he runs the risk of antagonising Dante, he still wants to assist his son. This positive representation of single fatherhood is quite rare in society and so Blackman uses Tyler as a way of showing that fathers can be as supportive as mothers (5).

Arguably, however (6), some readers may see Tyler's style of parenting in a negative way, especially when he is almost dismissive of Dante's outstanding achievement, 'So you managed to pass, did you?' Tyler also makes a number of judgements about Dante and the fact he has become a 'cliché' by getting a girl pregnant in his teens, reflecting society's negative viewpoint about teenage parents (7). Nevertheless, Tyler tells Dante that there is 'no shame' in doing any job if it is to provide for your family, suggesting that Tyler knows Dante may experience prejudice about being a young father who is forced to take a minimum wage job owing to his lack of experience and qualifications, and wants to ensure that his son knows he will not be one that judges him (8).

Interestingly, Blackman draws attention to the fact that Tyler and Dante are similar on a number of occasions in the novel, perhaps to reflect the idea that children often imitate their parents. However, Dante changes Tyler's words, saying 'Boys don't cry, but real men do.' By recasting this phrase at the end of the novel, Blackman may be trying to reflect how the younger generation of men are starting to challenge the ideas of toxic masculinity that the older generation, represented by Tyler, are struggling to escape (9).

1. Premise firmly establishes the intentions of the author (AO3) and the focus on the question. (AO1)
2. Layered comments about context are integrated into the essay. (AO3)
3. Perceptive discussion about the title. (AO1)
4. Range of focused references and shows how Blackman has used the character. (AO1) Also uses sophisticated punctuation for effect. (AO4)
5. Exploration of societal views. (AO3)
6. Consideration of alternative viewpoints can add to the critical style of an essay. (AO1) Also uses a range of paragraph starts to clarify argument. (AO4)
7. Contextual ideas are woven into the points. (AO3)
8. Wide range of textual references and an assured personal response. (AO1)
9. Perceptive final argument that fully links the response to context. (AO1 and AO3)

Questions

EXAM PRACTICE

Spend 50 minutes planning, writing and proofreading a response to one of the character questions on pages 58–61.

Planning a Theme Question Response

You must be able to: understand what an exam question is asking you and prepare your response.

How might an exam question be phrased?

Theme questions are structured in a similar way to the character questions:

'Whether you give her up or keep her, your world has now changed and it's going to stay that way.' (Tyler)

Explain the significance of change in the novel.

You **must** refer to the context of the novel in your answer.

[40 marks] (includes 8 marks for the range of appropriate vocabulary and sentence structures, and accurate use of spelling and punctuation)

How do I work out what to do?

Just like with character questions, theme questions require you to construct a cohesive argument that explores how the theme is important to both the narrative and the message that Blackman is trying to convey.

You will still need to ensure that you cover the three assessment objectives and so you will need to ensure that you give yourself sufficient time to proofread your response.

How do I prepare for a theme question?

For theme questions, you need to think about how and why Blackman uses the themes she does and how they are important in the novel. You will also need to think about the scenes in the novel which reflect these themes. Remember, you may not always be given the most obvious themes to focus on.

Both theme questions and character questions are seen as equally challenging by the exam board so go for the question that you feel you can answer the most successfully.

What should my plan look like?

Theme questions are assessed in the same way as character questions and so you will need to plan in a similar way. You will need to identify five or six points and think carefully about the order of your points to ensure you produce a cohesive argument.

For theme questions, you might want to start by establishing why the theme is important straightaway. The opening lines of an essay, where you frame your main argument, is called a **premise**.

For theme questions, you might want to think about how you could use your premise to establish your argument. For example, in the change question above, you might want to focus on how change is shown using one specific character or by looking at a particular event in the text.

Sample premises

Blackman shows that change is a significant theme as the protagonist in the novel experiences a completely life-changing moment when he discovers he is a father.

For this premise, the essay will focus on how change is shown through Dante's experiences and discuss how change is shown to be important.

One of the most significant moments that causes change in the novel is the attack on Adam. The attack has a huge impact on all the characters and causes a huge change in the tone of the novel.

For this premise, the essay will focus on a specific event and how that has caused significant change within the novel. Again, it is important that the focus of the essay is on the changes caused by the attack and not the attack itself.

Change is a central theme in the novel as all the characters experience things which cause significant changes in their lives.

This premise is a more general argument and proposes the idea that change is central to the novel. The fact that the premise is quite broad will give the writer the opportunity to explore a number of different moments or scenes in the novel.

Summary

- Revise both major and minor themes in the novel.
- You can adapt theme questions to cover a very specific focus or a broader focus.
- Theme questions are assessed in the same way as character questions and require the same skills.

Questions

1. How are theme questions similar to character questions?
2. Why doesn't it matter whether you choose a theme or character question in the exam?
3. What is a premise?

Grade 5 Annotated Response to a Theme Question

'Whether you give her up or keep her, your world has now changed and it's going to stay that way.' (Tyler)

Explore the significance of change within the novel.

You **must** refer to the context of the novel in your answer.

[40 marks] (includes 8 marks for the range of appropriate vocabulary and sentence structures, and accurate use of spelling and punctuation)

Blackman opens the novel with a moment that will potentially change Dante's future. He is waiting for his A level results (1). The fact that this theme is presented at the start of the narrative helps to establish that this is a very significant theme throughout the novel (2).

Blackman wanted to try and produce a realistic novel that typical teenagers could relate to. By starting with a teenage character who feels nervous about their results and the impact they could have on his life, Blackman is able to effectively create a real feel to the novel (3).

Dante lists all the positive ways his life is going to change. By doing this Blackman is able to make the impact of Emma's arrival much more dramatic for the reader (4). Dante dreams of being successful so that his 'family wouldn't have to scratch for every penny.' However, Emma's arrival changes that and he is left claiming benefits in order to support his daughter and being anxious about money. By doing this (5), Blackman emphasises his anxiety by repeatedly using the motif of money throughout the text, potentially to ensure that readers are aware of how expensive raising a child actually is (6).

As well as wanting to show the realities of raising a child, Blackman also wanted to reflect the way that having a child changes people's lives and priorities (7). At the start of the novel, Dante appears to be quite selfish as he is only worried about how Emma's arrival will affect him and his plans. When his father says that they will all 'have to live with the consequences of [his] actions', Dante is shown to still only question how he is going to be able to go to university with a child and seems determined to give Emma away. Dante is initially unwilling to adjust his plans despite his father's assurances that his 'world has now changed'. (8)

However, by the end of the novel, Dante is shown to have embraced (9) the changes that have happened in his life and accepts that his initial plans will have to change as a result of Emma's arrival. Blackman shows that Dante is 'happy' and realises that having his family around him is what truly matters. Blackman may have tried to end the novel in this way to prove that even changes that seem frightening and overwhelming in the beginning can be hugely positive if you are able to embrace them (10).

1. Opening line is a little descriptive but is focused on the question. (AO1)
2. A direct reference to the theme in the context of the text itself. (AO3)
3. Clear discussion of authorial intent (AO3) but it is somewhat isolated and could be integrated into the response more. It is also expressed in quite simple and almost repetitive terms which could affect the AO4 marks.
4. Clear use of a range of relevant references to the text and the **expanded noun phrase** 'the positive ways' helps to show a personal response. (AO1)
5. There is a repetitive use of the phrase 'By doing this' which makes the essay sound less sophisticated. A variety of sentences is needed to secure AO4 marks.
6. An attempt to refer to a more complex device as a way of writing more critically. (AO1) However, this is not as focused on the question as it could be.
7. A relevant piece of context linked to authorial intent. (AO3)
8. Although there are clear links to the question and some relevant references to the text, the response is in danger of simply retelling the story here.
9. Trying to use more adventurous vocabulary will help gain marks for AO4.
10. There is a focused closing statement about how Blackman has used the theme of change. (AO1)

Questions

EXAM PRACTICE

Choose a paragraph or section from this essay. Read it through a few times then try to rewrite and improve it. You might:

- improve the sophistication of the language or the clarity of expression
- integrate the contextual points more fluently
- try to increase the range of punctuation and variety of sentence structures
- make sure the response avoids being too narrative.

Grade 7+ Annotated Response to a Theme Question

A proportion of the best top-band answers will be awarded Grade 8 or Grade 9. To achieve this, you should aim for a sophisticated, fluent and nuanced response that displays flair and originality.

'Whether you give her up or keep her, your world has now changed and it's going to stay that way.' (Tyler)

Explore the significance of change within the novel.

You **must** refer to the context of the novel in your answer.

[40 marks] (includes 8 marks for the range of appropriate vocabulary and sentence structures, and accurate use of spelling and punctuation)

Blackman immediately highlights that change will be a significant theme throughout the novel by opening with an event that will potentially change the protagonist's future: the arrival of his A level results (1). The inclusion of this event reflects the fact that Boys Don't Cry *fits into the realism genre (2) as it is a common rite of passage for many teenagers. Furthermore, the use of Dante's anxious internal monologue (3) helps emphasise how much power he believes his A levels have to impact on the rest of his life, enabling Blackman to effectively create an authentic tone within the opening chapter.*

Blackman also uses Dante's positive thoughts about how his life is going to change as a way of making Emma's arrival significantly more dramatic. The reader is fully informed of everything Dante stands to lose when the mantle of fatherhood is thrust upon him. Blackman deliberately (4) wanted to show that being a parent is a serious role and one that Dante initially struggles to accept.

A pivotal moment in the novel, when Dante changes his opinion of Emma, is embedded in a scene which initially highlighted Dante's refusal to concede that his life has had to change (5). When he takes Emma with him to Bar Belle, Logan insults her and calls her 'ugly'. Blackman uses this moment as a catalyst for making Dante claim her as his daughter. The emotional and public declaration that Dante makes helps emphasise the changing relationship between Dante and his daughter.

Blackman uses the changing relationship between Dante and Emma (6) as a way of illustrating how Dante's character develops and changes throughout the novel, again reinforcing how significant the theme is to the narrative (7). At the beginning of the novel, Dante is presented as a somewhat selfish character, as shown by the fact that he is only focused on how Emma's arrival affects him despite the fact that his father explicitly states that the whole family 'will have to live with the consequences of [his] actions.' Dante also fails to thank his father for purchasing items for Emma, further highlighting his self-centred nature (8).

The act of thanking his father later in the novel allows Blackman to illustrate that not only has Dante changed as a person but also helps to show how Emma has changed the relationship between father and son in a positive way. Dante thanks his father while they are all on an outing to the park – an event which is a significant change from their usual routine (9) suggesting that Emma's presence has brought the family together.

Finally, Blackman exaggerates how much Dante has changed by showing that he ends the novel feeling 'happy', almost the antithesis of how he felt at the start of the text (10). He realises that having his family around him is what truly matters. Blackman's personal experience of having children caused her to reflect on the way their presence forces you to re-evaluate your priorities and so this may have been the reason that she shows Dante embracing his role within the family in such a joyful way (11).

1. The opening line is fully focused on the question (AO1) and uses a more sophisticated and complex sentence structure. (AO4)
2. A reference to the literary context (AO3) of the novel is fully integrated into the analysis.
3. Literary terminology is used to increase the sophistication of the response. (AO1) Using technical terms also helps increase your (AO4) marks.
4. The use of the **adverb** helps to create a personal response as well as an evaluative tone about the writer's craft. (AO1)
5. A carefully selected reference is used to support the argument. (AO1)
6. Clear link between paragraphs creates a fluent and cohesive response. (AO1)
7. Explicit links back to the question help emphasise how focused the response is on the exam question. (AO1)
8. Using more than one reference from the text helps to make the point more convincing. (AO1)
9. This is an example of integrating the internal context of the text into the essay. (AO3)
10. By connecting the beginning and the end of the essay, there is a strong sense of structure. (AO1)
11. Notice how every paragraph, even the final one, has a link to context. (AO3)

Questions

EXAM PRACTICE

Spend 50 minutes planning, writing and proofreading a response to one of the theme questions on pages 58–61.

Glossary

acerbic – sharp or sarcastic; used to describe tone or manner.

admonish – to warn, reprimand or tell someone off.

adverb – a word which describes a verb or adjective.

antagonistic – showing feelings of hostility towards someone; deliberately irritating someone else through behaviour or language.

antithesis – the direct opposite; can be used to describe people or things.

bildungsroman – a genre of writing which follows the main protagonist from youth into adulthood; a coming-of-age story.

catalyst – a person or thing which triggers a dramatic event or change.

cohesive – if an essay is cohesive, all elements work well together and there is a strong sense of fluency.

confidante – a trusted person you can tell your secrets to.

connotations – associated meanings; interpretations which go beyond the literal meaning.

contraction – words such as 'don't' or 'can't' that are shortened versions of one or more words.

conventions – typical features or aspects of something.

derogatory – critical, negative or disrespectful; often used to describe tone, manner or language.

determiner – a type of word that shows what type of reference the noun has (such as 'the', 'a', 'some', 'many').

dramatic irony – a situation where the audience knows more than the characters.

dual narrative – a narrative which is told from two different perspectives.

exclamation – a sentence type which expresses heightened emotions such as surprise, shock or joy.

expanded noun phrase – a phrase of words typically made up of a determiner, an adjective and a noun.

extended metaphor – a metaphor that is developed by using multiple examples within a text.

family drama – a genre of writing that focuses on the conflicts and issues within everyday family life.

first-person narrative – a narrative that is told from that character's perspective; typically uses the pronouns 'I' and 'me'.

foil – typically used to describe a character who has very different values compared with the protagonist; can be used to refer to minor characters with the same qualities.

foreshadowing – warning about or indicating a future event.

intensifier – a type of adverb which emphasises an adjective (such as 'really', 'very').

intermediary – someone who acts as a link between two people to help them resolve conflict and come to an agreement.

internal monologue – the internal conversations people have in their own minds.

linear structure – a story which is told from start to finish in the order events happen.

literary realism – a genre of writing which focuses on elements of people's real experiences; often used to show the experiences of working and lower middle-class people.

motif – a recurring theme, image or symbol which is featured frequently in the text.

parallels – to draw parallels between two ideas is to show the ways in which they are similar.

pejorative – a type of word which expresses contempt, hatred or disapproval.

premise – the introductory part of an essay which establishes the main argument.

pronoun – a word that can be used in place of a noun (such as 'I', 'he', 'she', 'it').

protagonist – the main character within a story.

simile – a piece of figurative language that compares one thing to another, typically using 'like' or 'as'.

slur – as a noun, slur means an insult or a word designed to damage someone's reputation.

speech tag – the verb or adverb which indicates how a character says something in the text (such as 'hissed', 'bellowed', 'whispered').

stigma – a mark of disgrace; negative connotations across society.

stock phrases – phrases used frequently by a certain group of people.

subplot – a secondary plot within a novel.

surrogate parents – surrogacy refers to the act of someone carrying a baby for someone else; this is typically because one person is unable to have children any other way.

symbolic – a word, idea or item that is used to represent a broader idea.

tag question – a question which is tagged on to the end of a statement in typical conversation; can be used to express sarcasm, seek agreement and/or engage the other person in conversation.

transient – something which only lasts for a short time.

widower – a man whose spouse has died.

Answers

Pages 4–5

QUICK TEST

1. He wants to go to university.
2. Melanie says she has to run some errands.
3. An incident in a sports match against another school.
4. He gets four A-star results and he is younger than his peers.
5. He calls Emma 'it' and retreats to his room when she cries.

EXAM PRACTICE

Analysis might focus on: the pronouns Dante uses to describe Emma and how they change, reflecting his initial struggles with being a father; examples of how the insults that Adam and Dante use towards each other, showing they care about each other, help establish the genre; how the assertive tone that Tyler uses towards Adam and his supportive/caring actions help establish the relationship between the characters; how the way Dante sees his achievement as something better than that of his friends helps establish aspects of his character.

Pages 6–7

QUICK TEST

1. He feels awkward.
2. He appears unimpressed.
3. Disappointment and anger.
4. He is still talking about going to university and talks about fostering or adoption.
5. He bonds instantly with her.

EXAM PRACTICE

Analysis might focus on: Tyler's insistence that Dante takes responsibility; the phrase 'no shame' suggesting that family is important; how Adam's instant bond with Emma is shown; Dante's refusal to accept the impact she will have; a comparison of how Adam and Dante respond to her arrival; Tyler's anger and disappointment.

Pages 8–9

QUICK TEST

1. He is trying to get rid of his daughter and not many parents put their own children into care.
2. Since he was 13.
3. For not thanking his father for the purchases he made for Emma.
4. He is almost envious as he doesn't think he will get to be a father.
5. He is in denial about the impact Emma will have and is convinced the DNA results will show she is not his daughter.

EXAM PRACTICE

Analysis might include: use of the intensifier 'too young' to show Dante as an older brother who refuses to accept Adam's identity; the future tense 'will ever be' suggests Dante believes he will always be a failure in Tyler's eyes and helps develop their complex relationship; how Dante begins to feel the importance of being a father because the word goes 'so deep'.

Pages 10–11

QUICK TEST

1. He buys special porridge and goat's milk.
2. To celebrate the end of term and his exam results.
3. It is unclean and unsafe for Emma.
4. Logan calls Emma 'ugly'.
5. He was punched in the face – the reader assumes it was Josh who hit him but he doesn't tell anyone.

EXAM PRACTICE

Analysis might include: connotations of the word 'belongs' and how Dante's and Tyler's views contrast; Dante's blunt threat towards Logan – use of the modal verb 'will' suggests certainty to the threat; adjective 'stuck' has negative connotations and suggests Collette feels that Emma is a burden.

Pages 12–13

QUICK TEST

1. They talk about their plans and the future, but not about Emma.
2. She has had four miscarriages and cannot have children.
3. He sees it as Dante attempting to avoid his responsibility.
4. Tyler confesses that he feels redundant and he and Dante seem to resolve their differences.
5. The person he is with feels ashamed of his sexuality.

EXAM PRACTICE

Analysis might include: Dante feeling that women talk about their feelings but men should not; Tyler accusing Dante of trying to get rid of his responsibility like a lot of other men; the idea that men are critical and harsh to one another; Adam's partner being ashamed of his sexuality – links between masculinity and heterosexuality could be discussed.

Pages 14–15

QUICK TEST

1. Veronica says Social Services might consider taking Emma away from Dante.
2. She is staying with him.
3. He was not willing to be with someone who is ashamed of him and wants him to be in the shadows.
4. Because there is almost a fight and Logan, Josh and Paul are behaving badly.
5. They leave him with the bill.

EXAM PRACTICE

Analysis might include: the subtle way Veronica threatens Dante; the feelings of powerlessness Dante experiences; the contrast between the authority and power of Social Services and Dante's lack of power; the abusive and homophobic language Josh uses in Bar Belle; the reaction of Dante to the incident with Josh and Adam.

Pages 16–17

QUICK TEST

1. It happened when Dante and Adam were nearly home and away from Bar Belle.
2. Adam kisses Josh.
3. Everything, including the names of the attackers.
4. His face has been badly beaten: his eye socket and jaw are broken.
5. Because Adam was wanted/planned and he was not.

EXAM PRACTICE

Analysis might include: the way Logan insults Dante; the fact that the attack destroys the friendships Dante had; the protective way that Dante behaves towards Adam; the fact that Dante would go to prison for his brother; the way Blackman presents the trigger point for Josh; the fact that Adam is so unrecognisable afterwards and the impact this could have on his future career aspirations.

Pages 18–19

QUICK TEST

1. He has lied about his grades and has not got into university.
2. He says that Dante hates gay people as much as he does.
3. He is in constant pain, cannot sleep and has isolated himself from his family.
4. She kisses his scars and hugs him.
5. The visit is a success and Veronica has given them some good advice.

EXAM PRACTICE

Analysis might include: use of withholding information in Adam's relationship; the impact of Tyler withholding information from Dante and what happens when Dante finds out; the twist regarding Josh's sexuality; Melanie's act of keeping Emma a secret from Dante.

Pages 20–21

QUICK TEST

1. She keeps crying and demanding to go to the park even when he says no.
2. They see it as a sign of weakness.
3. Adam was upset about the loss of his good looks and his prospective career. He also misses his mother.
4. Dante and Adam share the same kind of banter.
5. He realises family is the most important thing.

EXAM PRACTICE

Ideas might include: analysing the way Dante changes his attitude towards Emma; how Dante matures over the course of the novel; the changing behaviour of Adam over the course of the novel and how his family reacts to his sexuality; how Tyler becomes more open with his sons about his feelings.

Pages 22–23

QUICK TEST

1. It is a narrative told from the first-person perspective of two different characters.
2. He has the majority of the chapters and his chapters are generally longer.
3. It allows the readers to understand how the narrators are feeling but also shows how few of these feelings they share.
4. Dante matures and takes on more responsibility; he moves into adulthood.
5. Literary realism and family drama.

EXAM PRACTICE

Ideas might include: analysing ways that Dante is shown to mature and develop as part of a bildungsroman; discussion of current affairs/issues that link it to realism; analysis of the domestic setting and central relationships for family drama.

Pages 24–25

QUICK TEST

1. The setting of the home reflects the literary realism and the family drama genres.
2. Dante wants to leave it and Adam sees it as somewhere special.
3. The net curtains are dirty and the kitchen is not very clean.
4. Dante takes more care over the kitchen and home to make things safe for Emma; it shows he is caring for her.
5. Dante originally sees the bar as a lively place but with Emma he sees the negative side of it.

EXAM PRACTICE

Analysis about the home might include: the links between the setting and the genre; how Blackman uses the changes in the home to echo the changes in the family; how Blackman uses the home to show the differences between the narrators.

Analysis about Bar Belle might include: how the bar reflects Dante's changing attitudes towards fatherhood; how the bar is instrumental in showing the division between Dante and his friends; how Bar Belle is used to symbolise youth and to reflect Dante's maturity.

Pages 26–27

QUICK TEST

1. Dante observes that education provides opportunities to get better jobs and earn better money.
2. Melanie had to give up college to have Emma and Dante is having to give up university. It suggests that teen pregnancy means people cannot continue with their education.
3. Because teen pregnancy in the UK is at a very high rate.
4. Tyler calls Dante an 'idiot' for getting Melanie pregnant and a stranger calls Dante a 'waster'.
5. Adam is openly gay and proud of his sexuality whereas Josh is ashamed and keeps it a secret.

EXAM PRACTICE

Ideas might include: links between the fact this is a Young Adult novel and the presentation of education; Collette's determination to make something of her life, suggesting that anyone without an education cannot do this; the impact Emma has on both Melanie's and Dante's ability to continue education; the contrast between Josh and Adam regarding LGBTQ+ issues; an exploration of how attitudes towards teen pregnancy are presented.

Pages 28–29

QUICK TEST

1. Twenty-first century.
2. Josh uses 'gay' as a pejorative term and the campaign aimed at stopping that.
3. Laws about homosexual couples using surrogates were not passed until 2010, when the book was published.
4. There was perceived bias towards fathers in law and the courts.
5. Dante's inability to find a job reflects the high unemployment rate. Dante is frequently worried about money.

EXAM PRACTICE

Ideas might include: analysis of how Blackman presents ideas about masculinity; how Blackman uses and/or challenges stereotypes; how the context reinforces the literary realism genre; how bias against teenage fathers is shown; how Josh's homophobia is presented and the consequences of ignoring his hate speech.

Answers

Pages 30–31

QUICK TEST

1. She felt that books about teen pregnancy were only told from a female perspective and she wanted to explore the other side.
2. She shows children can be relentlessly demanding and highlights Dante's lack of sleep, his worries about money, etc.
3. Blackman has a child and found it difficult despite being in her thirties when she had her daughter. She has three brothers who found it hard to talk about their feelings.
4. Men consider talking about feelings to be a feminine trait.
5. There was an increase in homophobic crimes at the time of writing.

EXAM PRACTICE

Analysis might include: ideas about how positively Dante is presented as he changes; how severe the attack on Adam is; how Dante reflects the difficulties of being a parent; the way Tyler talks about being a parent; the difficulty the male characters have in terms of talking about their feelings.

Pages 32–33

QUICK TEST

1. He gets four A-stars in his exams despite being only 17.
2. He argues with his brother, he is nervous about his results and he is desperate to leave home.
3. Tyler is dismissive of Dante's achievements.
4. He refuses to believe it when Melanie tells him Emma is his daughter. He calls Emma 'it'.

EXAM PRACTICE

Analysis might include: Dante's long-term plans, shown by the intensifying phrase 'way beyond'; how his questioning of Melanie shows his disbelief; the physical action of 'swallowing' suggests that Dante is extremely upset by Tyler's dismissal – it implies he is repressing his emotions.

Pages 34–35

QUICK TEST

1. Up until that point, Dante has pretended Emma is a relative.
2. By withdrawing his confirmation before knowing the result, Dante shows he plans to care for Emma regardless; this also suggests he has accepted that she is his.
3. Dante loses his temper and nearly hits Emma. He also asks Aunt Jackie for help and opens up about his fears.

EXAM PRACTICE

Analysis might include: the use of the possessive pronoun 'my' to show he claims her as his; the structure of events and the timing of the withdrawal from university shows he accepts his daughter and his responsibilities – could link to bildungsroman genre; the violent connotations of 'hitting' and Dante's accompanying sense of shame.

Pages 36–37

QUICK TEST

1. Both Dante and Adam have clear plans for the future.
2. He uses the exclamation 'Wow!' to show he is excited.
3. When Emma kisses his scars, she reminds Adam of his mother, who he misses. This makes him feel isolated and lonely.

EXAM PRACTICE

Analysis might include: his confidence with his sexuality and the conflict this causes with his family; his belief after the attack that his looks are appalling as shown by the noun 'nightmares'; the contrast between his confidence at the beginning and his nervousness and fear at the end of the novel.

Pages 38–39

QUICK TEST

1. He is a widower – his wife died.
2. He takes time off work to care for them and buys things for Emma.
3. Tyler is dismissive of Dante's achievements but does offer to come home to support him after Veronica's visit.

EXAM PRACTICE

Ideas might include: analysis of Tyler's actions that show he supports his family; exploration of how and when Tyler tells his sons he loves them; the fact that Tyler offers to help even though he knows it is a 'risk'; the way Dante learns to appreciate his father's help.

Pages 40–41

QUICK TEST

1. Her arrival causes a lot of dramatic changes to all the characters.
2. Dante experiences a lot of prejudice because he is a male parent and a lot of characters talk about the stereotype of men abandoning their children.
3. Emma highlights the prejudice against young parents. She also highlights the difficulty of being a parent.

EXAM PRACTICE

Analysis might include: the idea that children belong to their parents; Tyler's use of the adjective 'inconvenient' shows his anger at Dante for wanting to give Emma up; exploration of the love between parents and children; the verb 'clung' suggests a deep connection; ideas contrasting 'house' and 'home' – explicit references to the positive impact Emma has had.

Pages 42–43

QUICK TEST

1. Her mother has kicked her out and her aunt will only let her stay if she gives up Emma. Her father didn't stick around.
2. She doesn't anticipate the confrontation or prejudice Dante experiences when she tells people Emma is his.
3. That men cannot talk about their feelings or ask for help.
4. She represents the idea that Emma could be taken from Dante.

EXAM PRACTICE

Ideas might include: the contrast between Melanie and Dante; the way Collette could be seen as a foil for both Dante and Melanie; Collette's views towards Emma and how they both reflect and contrast with Dante's changing views; Jackie as a confidante and the way she represents gender stereotypes; Veronica as a device used to create tension.

Pages 44–45

QUICK TEST

1. Josh defended him from some bullies.
2. Dante is successful and Logan thinks Dante believes he is better than their group of friends.
3. He believes the attack wouldn't have happened if it had not been for Logan winding Josh up.

EXAM PRACTICE

Analysis might include: discussion about Josh's language and links to the Stonewall campaign; the presentation of Logan as cruel and manipulative; the contrast between Josh as a defender of Dante but also a bully of others.

Pages 46–47

QUICK TEST

1. Dante is unable to talk to his friends because of Emma.
2. Adam's friends are mostly girls and they let Adam shine, whereas Dante's predominantly male friendship group seems to make him uncomfortable. He has had to change himself.
3. Both friendship groups stop calling when things get difficult.
4. Logan threatens Josh's masculinity.
5. Dante changes parts of his identity to suit Josh. Josh is racist and this makes Dante cringe.

EXAM PRACTICE

Analysis might include: the unequal relationship between Josh and Dante as Dante adjusts to suit Josh; the stereotypes surrounding LGBTQ+ men and the attitude that Dante has towards Adam's female friendships; the way friendship is used to reflect the challenges parenthood creates for Dante.

Pages 48–49

QUICK TEST

1. Dante would attack Wolverine if he threatened Adam.
2. The strained relationship between her and Tyler appears resolved as they are all happy at the end.
3. Melanie says she is 'scared' of what she might do if she is left alone with Emma any longer.
4. The petty banter and care for each other reflects a realistic view of families. Blackman also shows the reality of being a parent.
5. Not being a good enough father to Emma.

EXAM PRACTICE

Analysis might include: the expectations on parents and how they should treat their children; the importance of a family network; the contrast between Melanie and Dante in terms of the support they have; the changing relationship between parents and children within the novel.

Pages 50–51

QUICK TEST

1. He talks about money a lot and it is a reason for him wanting a good job.
2. He repeats how he has no money to look after Emma and worries about it at a number of points.
3. It shows he is supportive of Dante and excited to be a grandparent.
4. Because it is her tax money being used to provide welfare support to unemployed parents.
5. The impact of the 2008 financial crisis can be seen in the novel.

EXAM PRACTICE

Ideas might include: the way Dante lists no money as the first issue when it comes to supporting Emma; the motif of money throughout the novel to reflect Dante's fears; the issues surrounding the use of the welfare system and prejudices associated with people on benefits.

Pages 52–53

QUICK TEST

1. That men abandon their children and that they cannot talk about their feelings.
2. It implies that men should not show fear or emotion and should have a practical approach to things.
3. He wants to be an actor.
4. He has lost his good looks and his confidence.
5. To emphasise that it is not a significant part of the story.

EXAM PRACTICE

Ideas might include: Dante's presentation of men and women as different; the frequency of characters mentioning male stereotypes; Dante's anger at the prejudice he suffers; the way Josh is used to illustrate and reflect different ideas about identity.

Pages 54–55

QUICK TEST

1. There is a stigma around teenage pregnancy and her mother threw her out of the house.
2. Adam is open about his sexuality whereas Josh keeps his sexuality a secret.
3. Parenting – because both Melanie and Tyler keep secrets from Dante about how and when they became parents; identity – because Josh keeps his sexuality a secret; masculinity – the male members of the Bridgeman family keep their feelings secret from one another.
4. Melanie is thrown out of her home. She cannot go to school.
5. Josh keeps his sexuality a secret because he feels it threatens his masculinity.

EXAM PRACTICE

Ideas might include: the dramatic impact of Melanie keeping her location a secret from Dante; the impact Josh's secret has on himself and others; discussions about the dramatic effect of how Dante finds out about his mother and father's marriage.

Pages 62–63

Questions

1. AO1, AO3 and AO4.
2. The social and historical context of the novel, the writer's intentions, and the context of the novel itself.
3. Because accuracy is worth 20% of the marks.

Pages 64–65

EXAM PRACTICE

Sample Upgrade of Paragraph 1

Tyler is the father in the novel and, as the novel focuses on fathers, this shows he is an important character. Blackman emphasises Tyler's importance by using one of his lines as the title. The phrase 'boys don't cry' helps illustrate how men are supposed to repress their feelings, something which all the male characters do throughout the novel. Blackman may have shown Tyler using controversial phrases like 'boys don't cry' and 'man up' as a way of presenting ideas about toxic masculinity, which were highly significant at the time Blackman was writing.

Additional points could include: discussion about how Tyler is used to present Dante maturing, with links to the bildungsroman genre; exploration of the way Blackman draws parallels between Tyler's experience and Dante's experience and how this might reflect the common challenges all parents face.

Pages 66–67

EXAM PRACTICE

Use the mark scheme on page 80 to self-assess your strengths and weaknesses. Work up from the bottom, putting a tick by things you have fully accomplished, a ½ by skills that are in place but need securing, and underlining areas that need particular development. The estimated grade boundaries are included so you can assess your progress towards your target grade.

Answers

Pages 68–69

1. You need to construct a cohesive argument that looks at the importance of the theme to the narrative and the message of the book.
2. The exam board sees them as equally important.
3. The opening lines of an essay that frame your argument.

Pages 70–71

EXAM PRACTICE

Sample Upgrade of Paragraph 3

While waiting for his A level results, Dante lists all the positive ways his life is going to change. One of these ways is the fact that Dante will be successful enough to ensure that his 'family wouldn't have to scratch for every penny.' Incorporating a large amount of specific detail into this scene allows Blackman to make Emma's arrival more dramatic as her presence completely derails Dante's plans. Dante continually worries about money throughout the novel, especially when he is left claiming benefits in order to support his daughter. By using the recurring motif of money, and specifically money worries, Blackman is able to emphasise how expensive raising a child actually is, reinforcing the realism genre of the text.

Pages 72–73

EXAM PRACTICE

Use the mark scheme below to self-assess your strengths and weaknesses. Work up from the bottom, putting a tick by things you have fully accomplished, a ½ by skills that are in place but need securing, and underlining areas that need particular development. The estimated grade boundaries are included so you can assess your progress towards your target grade.

Grade	AO1	AO3	AO4
6–7+	Response is assured and confident with precisely selected references to support ideas. There is a convincing and perceptive style to the essay.	Excellent understanding of the influence of context. Links between context and the text are perceptive and integrated into the main body of the essay.	A broad range of vocabulary and punctuation that is used almost flawlessly. Sentence structure adds to the meaning and is used for effect. Writing is controlled and sophisticated.
4–5	Response has a secure structure and presents a clear argument that is focused on the question. Style is generally appropriate and there are a number of supporting references.	Secure discussion about context with relevant focused links between context and the text.	Spelling and punctuation is considerably accurate. There is a considerable range of vocabulary and sentence structures. Writing is controlled.
2–3	A narrative style of essay with some references to the text. Style loses focus in places and does not maintain tone.	Some comment about context although not always focused on the question. Some attempt to link the context and the novel together.	A reasonable range of vocabulary and punctuation that is generally accurate. Some variety of sentence structure and punctuation.